AHSA ®

BAL AGEING NETWORK

Architecture *for an*
Ageing Population

International Association of Homes and Services for the Ageing

Architecture *for an* Ageing Population

images
Publishing

Published in Australia in 2014 by
The Images Publishing Group Pty Ltd
ABN 89 059 734 431
6 Bastow Place, Mulgrave, Victoria 3170, Australia
Tel: +61 3 9561 5544 Fax: +61 3 9561 4860
books@imagespublishing.com
www.imagespublishing.com

National Library of Australia Cataloguing-in-Publication entry:

Title:	Architecture for an ageing population / International Association of Homes and Services for the Ageing (IAHSA).
ISBN:	9781864705188 (hbk.)
Subjects:	Architecture, domestic.
	Dwellings.
	Old age homes.
	Older people—Care.
Dewey number	728

Edited by Driss Fatih

Designed by The Graphic Image Studio Pty Ltd, Mulgrave, Australia
www.tgis.com.au

Pre-publishing services by United Graphic Pte Ltd, Singapore
Printed by Asia Pacific Offset in Hong Kong/China on 140 gsm Matt Art paper

IMAGES has included on its website a page for special notices in relation to this and our other publications.
Please visit www.imagespublishing.com.

Contents

Foreword

Good design influences quality of care, effectiveness of service delivery, efficiency of operations, and most importantly, quality of life. Design influences behavior, attitude, and activity. And design reflects the values of those who create it and their aspirations for what will transpire in the space.

The art and science of design for spaces used primarily by older people has progressed over the years. As we better understand the process of aging, adopt evidence-based practices, and listen carefully to consumers, the design of spaces designed for living, working, socializing, dining, and exercising has evolved. We are increasingly mindful of accessibility and color, but also of proximity, health, and wellness. Outdoor spaces are as important as spaces with a roof. The ability to socialize is widely understood to be an essential ingredient for a quality life. The needs of those with dementia as well as those who care for them drives design decisions. And an unabashed focus on the people who will occupy that space drives ideas about creating purpose as an essential dimension of design.

As we face an unprecedented demographic shift to a rapidly aging world, we have an obligation to consider broadly and deeply the kinds of environments we are creating. What will support the need for engagement, promote healthy lifestyles, accommodate frailty or disability, underscore the importance of family, and provide needed connections to community? What will facilitate teamwork and collaboration among staff? How do we translate research findings about the physiology of aging and evidence-based approaches to care and service delivery into design features? How do we create community out of carefully considered spaces?

Design for Ageing offers an international perspective on these issues, providing innovative solutions and approaches in a variety of settings. The designs push us to challenge our assumptions of aging, space, and what is possible. They cause us to pause and think about our own old age and how and where we might want to live. And they provide a sense of optimism that there are many who are truly committed not just to beautiful design, but to environments that understand and embrace the stage in life that we call aging.

Katrinka Smith Sloan
Executive Director,
International Association of Homes and Services for the Ageing (IAHSA)

Introduction

The designs featured in the following pages embody a commitment to creating space that focuses on facilitating a high quality of life. There are small-scale designs and large campuses. There are designs that address the needs of those with dementia, those living alone, those with active lifestyles, and those facing the challenges that often accompany ageing. There are designs that reposition existing communities, expansions, rural and urban settings, and communities of a range of sizes. There are small congregate environments, including cohousing. There are urban campuses that integrate with the community at large and those that are designed to become the community itself. There are luxury projects and those designed to serve a lower economic profile. Across all the designs, the common theme is one of appreciation for the needs and expectations of those for whom the space is designed—those in the later stages of life.

Redevelopment

Redevelopment of existing communities or campuses is done fairly routinely, as owners and providers of retirement living recognize the changing expectations of consumers. In some cases, development involves joining two contiguous communities into one, allowing for the expansion of services to meet a greater range of needs. In every case, the intent is to expand services while not duplicating options and amenities. The challenge of creating an integrated campus was achieved in both examples described below.

At Holy Spirit Westcourt, Bickerton Masters Architecture joined a retirement village and a nursing home to create a continuum of care. In doing so, it was important to maintain the community legacy embedded in its 41-year history of the Bethlehem Nursing Home, thereby preserving an important dimension of the organization's mission, supported by the Sisters of Mercy and the Diocese of Cairns.

Beyond providing a more integrated array of services for residents, Holy Spirit Westcourt had a strategic goal of creating a focal point not only for the Catholic community in Cairns but for the general community in this suburb. Community facilities such as the café and chapel are open to the public and the other amenities such as the gym and hair salon provide opportunities for local business to extend their operations to the Holy Spirit Westcourt residents.

Similarly, Air Force Villages by Perkins Eastman initiated a repositioning of its two self-contained campuses—one location offering an urban lifestyle and the other a rural setting. The strategic intent was to focus on addressing the future marketability of housing options and amenities for residents. It was crucial that the plan address resident preferences at each campus. Air Force Village also wished to redesign their long-term care space and replace their existing model of care with a smaller-scale, more intimate, residential model. The resulting plan integrated the campuses, allowing each to stand as a neighborhood within a larger combined context of the Air Force Villages' community.

Campus Communities

Campus Communities are ambitious projects done on a large scale. They take advantage of the land to which they have access and are rich with amenities and options for their residents. In some cases, such as Taube Koret Campus for Jewish Life, the campus serves a range of needs and interests across generations. The addition of apartments for the elderly, designed by Steinberg Architects, adds a broader purpose to an existing campus. In Shenyang, China, a comprehensive master plan for Union Life Shenyang Retirement Community was designed by LRS Architects. As planned, this project will be the largest, most comprehensive modern senior community in Northeast China. In Australia, the focus of Waterbrook Yowie Bay, designed by Campbell Luscombe Architects, is on luxury living in an unusually large parcel of land in a suburban setting. Similarly, three: living architecture's Solano at Cinco Ranch is located in a suburban community. In contrast, Huruan Shimei Bay Residences, also by three: living architecture, accentuates the natural beauty of the mountains and rivers that surround the campus.

In Shenyang, the initial phase is part of a three-phase master plan. Other phases will provide residential and community services for an independent resident population and will accommodate residents who need assisted, skilled, and memory care services. Each area will have clearly organized common areas, including their own kitchens. Lifestyle services include medical rehabilitation, nursing, health, leisure, and lifelong learning, all influenced by and woven into the local Chinese culture. The design aesthetics are based on traditional English manor-style architecture integrating references to late-medieval country homes to provide a timeless sense of place.

Both Taube Koret Campus for Jewish Life (above) and Union Life Campus in Shenyang have integrated an educational, cultural, recreational, and social dimension to campus structures. In Shenyang, a commercial and active senior lifestyle center is adjacent to the campus, reinforcing the vision of a multi-purpose, fully integrated community that will serve a wide range of needs as well as components that will help build a strong community. Connected to this by a footbridge are a temple, meditation hall, and lodge for monks arranged around a grand central park. The plan also calls for a separate medical building that will provide both Chinese and Western health services for residents of the campus and the community at large.

The Taube Koret Campus for Jewish Life (TKCJL) is a multi-generational campus that offers a wide range of educational, cultural, recreational, and social opportunities in a Jewish context. It combines proven urban design principles with architecture appropriate to the Silicon Valley in California. On the campus, the Jewish Community Center and the Jewish Home blend together, connecting both horizontally and vertically. Each of the eight houses for seniors is a unique community, built and connected to one another. By reducing scale, TKCJL hopes to foster engagement, including engagement across generations. By combining senior living with the community center and its many amenities, residents have access to a broad range of activities. A series of outdoor rooms make up the heart of the community, including a town square, cultural courtyard, children's courtyard, and senior housing courtyards.

The strategic intent of Waterbrook was to offer independent senior living in a high-quality resort environment, coupled with the services and facilities that residents would expect to find in a luxury hotel. The owner, Waterbrook Lifestyle Resorts, was quick to recognize the changing demographic (largely based on Sydney's rising property values) that would provide a market for retirement housing at the higher end of the economic spectrum. They selected a site close

to desirable property features and added landscaped gardens, two apartment buildings, and a garden clubhouse designed around a series of linked, secluded open spaces, focusing around a man-made, but totally naturalistic landscaped water feature that flows through the length of the resort. The style of the building was developed to respond to the memories of senior residents by utilizing a dignified contemporary interpretation of the "grand" classical apartment buildings of the 1920s and '30s. In contrast to other campus developments, it has a relatively small number of apartments—just 72—but the spaces are generous, giving it the feel of a complete and well-designed and integrated campus.

Huruan Shimei Bay Residences, designed by three: living architecture, is in a spectacular natural environment surrounded by forested mountains and two natural rivers flowing into the sea. The surrounding forest and rivers promote an atmosphere of health, wellness, and life. The pathway that traverses the site serves as a metaphor for the twists, turns, and changes that each individual experiences in life. The main pathway begins at the base of the mountain and meanders through the Commons or "heart" of the community, emptying into the retail plaza and connecting with the pedestrian path and roadway, which lead to other areas of Shimei Bay. The campus, designed around the goal of pedestrian circulation, reinforces the emphasis on wellness and holistic living to enhance the daily lives of the residents.

The campus of The Solana at Cinco Ranch, also designed by three: living architecture, is compact and efficient, with independent living and assisted living residences, common areas, and a series of outdoor courts that provide activities from dining to bocce to a resort pool and water feature. Cinco Ranch used a specific palette of exterior materials, from which a Texas urban style was crafted. Signature architectural designs include a rotunda and tower, which have been repeated on subsequent Solana projects nationwide. Cinco Ranch has 126 independent living apartments and 32 assisted living apartments.

Independent Living on a Small Scale

Projects designed for independent living on a small scale take many shapes and forms. From cohousing, designed and managed by the residents, to community-oriented independent living, to vertical living, small-scale projects respond to the desire for a home-like environment and the need to create community on a more intimate scale. Mountain View, by McCamant & Durrett Architects, is a rehabilitated farmhouse. Stillwater Senior Cohousing's buildings have no more than four units each. Valley View Senior Cohousing was built into the side of a hill, creating a sense of community through its terraced structure. THW's Cohen Rosen House and McCamant & Durrett's Wolf Creek Lodge are designed to reinforce the natural beauty in the area that surrounds them. Lifestyle Manor Bondi by Campbell Luscombe Architects in Australia brings luxury living in a small-scale high rise to a suburban community.

Cohousing is a grassroots movement that grows directly out of people's desire for an alternative to existing housing choices. Cohousing communities are unique in their extensive use of common space. They are organized, planned, and managed by the residents themselves. Each resident or household has a separate dwelling and chooses how much he or she wants to participate in community activities.

McCamant & Durrett has designed a number of small-scale residences, often in conjunction with a restored older building. Mountain View is a cohousing project consisting of a three-story building and a single-story, rehabilitated farmhouse with 19 residential units, a caregiver's apartment, a clubhouse and 39 underground parking spaces. Stillwater Cohousing, also known as Oakcreek, consists of six four-unit buildings and a single-story, rehabilitated brick house that serves as the common house. The 24 dwelling units are clustered into three eight-unit pods. Stillwater Senior Cohousing is also a senior cohousing community, allowing seniors to age-in-place.

Another cohousing project designed by McCamant & Durrett, Wolf Creek Lodge, completed in 2012, includes 30 one and two-bedroom independent condominiums ranging in size from 55 square meters to 100 square meters. The common areas include a large dining room, gourmet kitchen, sitting area with fireplace, laundry, office, crafts rooms, and three guests rooms, one of which may be used as caregiver quarters. Outside, there are community gardens and a spa, as well as 35 parking spaces in a variety of open and garage spaces. While the community itself is located on less than half a hectare, it is adjacent to a hectare of permanent open space along a mountain stream.

At Silver Sage Senior Cohousing, McCamant & Durrett's design focuses on creating a community that supports each resident with an emphasis on "Spiritual Eldering: nurturing and encouraging the desire to keep learning, growing and participating." By integrating community garden space, outdoor balconies, and walkways, a central staircase, common terrace, shared meals, proximity to downtown Boulder, and location within the Holiday Neighborhood, which is new and very eclectic, the residents are able to age-in-place. All these elements are meant to support meaningful interaction where the residents are inspired to learn, create, and share with each other.

Valley View Senior Housing is a McCamant & Durrett project that is an affordable, rental senior housing development on a 1.5-hectare site with 70 dwelling units, a clubhouse, open space, and parking. Valley View Senior Housing is 100 per cent rental housing. The site is sloped toward the east, creating a hillside town with meandering paths, electric vehicle charging stations, garden beds, bocce ball court, and a common terrace.

THW-designed Cohen-Rosen House has a non-institutional design approach and space that encourages interaction and connectivity with others and with nature. The exterior courtyard has water features, gardening tables, paths, and amenities to encourage outside activities. The design of the house encourages interaction with others through the informal open common areas that are used by all residents. The central living room and dining area are designed to be the heartbeat of the house. Artwork is installed throughout and the Art Room promotes both physical and mental activities, as well as opportunities to interact and work together on projects and activities that promote creativity and conversation.

Also a non-institutional design, Lifestyle Manor Bondi, designed by Campbell Luscombe Architects, is a luxury retirement apartment in the heart of Sydney's upscale eastern suburbs. The owners envisaged a retirement community that would enable their residents to experience the very best of city living, in a secure vibrant environment. The core of the development of 42 luxury, one, two, and three bedroom apartments is the glass-roofed central atrium passing through five of the building's seven levels, giving true life to the concept of the "vertical village." By internally revealing resident activity over five levels, the sense of physical, social, and

visual communication reinforces communality (the sense of "belonging") and creates a positive and activating atmosphere.

The development's facilities incorporate a rooftop dining room with terrace for entertaining, a lower-level cinema, gym, hair salon and treatment room, function center, arts and crafts workshop, medical consulting suite, heated swimming pool, and, on the main lobby level, a library and an intimate lounge space. The style of the building was developed to respond to the aesthetic aspirations and memories of senior residents by utilizing a dignified contemporary interpretation of the "grand" apartment buildings of the 1920s.

Continuing Care Retirement Communities

Continuing Care Retirement Communities (CCRC) are purposely built to meet a range of needs as people age. Their focus on the continuum provides a secure and supportive environment that recognizes that as people age, their needs may change. Because of the range of services offered, CCRCs are often on a campus. Rincon del Rio is one such campus. Designed by McCamant & Durrett, Rincon del Rio is a 345-unit senior living complex designed to serve 450 residents in South Nevada County. Located on 85 hectares along the Bear River, the project includes a variety of types of residential units in a campus setting that also includes community support services, recreational opportunities, farmland, and open space. Rincon del Rio is a CCRC, incorporating commercial space, private dwellings, and a cohousing community. The Village is designed to provide space to accommodate all the services and resources residents need to help them lead a fulfilling life at home.

Expansion

It is not uncommon for existing service providers to expand either their scope or size, or both. Several creative designs support this kind of expansion. Belong Wigan Village (above), designed by Pozzoni, has taken a care home and expanded it by adding independent living apartments. Lenbrook, an almost 40-year-old CCRC in Atlanta, has added both apartments and amenities to keep up with market demands. And, starting as a care home for 66 residents, Belong Wigan Village has added 54 independent living apartments to complete the Village. The emphasis is on maximizing independence as the residents age, while ensuring that their needs can be met. Belong Wigan Village provides 11 private ensuite rooms located within six small contemporary households that provide individuals with support and rehabilitation opportunities. Each house is safe and secure, with access to a garden or balcony. The 54 independent living apartments allow for an independent lifestyle within easy reach of the full services and amenities of the community. Residents live independently and are given opportunities to give care and support to others, as well as receive such care and support as needed or desired.

Lenbrook was conceived by an Atlanta businessman, who in the early 1980s determined to build an upscale, full-service retirement community in the attractive Buckhead neighborhood of Atlanta. The community opened to its first residents in July 1983. The original site sat on a 1.5- hectare plot and accommodated 225 residents. After 20 years, the owners wanted to ensure the continued success of the community by adding more convenience for the residents. Services and amenities were expanded with state-of-the-art modifications. Lenbrook received the necessary permits and funding to proceed with 142 new residences, a wellness center and spa, and the renovation of existing community areas. The owner acquired an adjacent land parcel of 1 hectare, allowing for the expansion.

Designs to Serve those with Dementia

A major challenge to the residential aged care community is that the necessarily large infrastructure needed to service the health and residential needs of frail, elderly people in an economically viable manner can become institutional and hospital-like. The solution employed by many architects is to disguise that infrastructure in support of the small-scale, homelike, and community-focused spaces. These can be smaller residential clusters, small intimate spaces or neighborhoods, with meals prepared in more intimate settings and common space close to residences. These design solutions foster a more person-centered approach to care and services and allow residents to maximize their independence.

Hammond Care's Miranda is designed to be a home for people with dementia. It is separated into eight small cottages with all the elements of home life—kitchen, laundry, living room, and garden. Four of the cottages have 15 single bedrooms, while the other four have just eight single bedrooms, which is unusual in Australia. The home-like atmosphere, including the cottages and singe rooms, lends itself to a more person-centered approach to care, respecting the dignity and privacy of the individual residents, as well as that of their residents' families.

The domestic environment within each cottage allows for natural encounters between staff and residents to reflect the rhythms of normal home life. The kitchen and living areas are a pivotal focal point within each household. There are no dead ends or blind corridors to facilitate ease of orientation for residents. Each cottage has its own secure garden area with a continuous path. To create a sense of identity and security, each home is differentiated in multiple ways, from the color of the roofing tiles, external brickwork and paints, and the door handles on residents' bedroom doors.

EachStep Blackley, designed by Pozzoni, is a pioneering, £5 million dementia service based in Manchester, UK, which offers a complete range of support for people with dementia—home care, day care, respite care, and residential and nursing care. By providing this holistic package of support from one central service, the community is able to support people with dementia each step of the way, in their own homes and with specialized services.

EachStep Blackley is a vibrant service organization where people are supported to be engaged and well cared for. The mental stimulation and physical wellbeing of those who access these services are attended to, ensuring that they remain part of their communities and follow the interests and activities they enjoy. The vision of EachStep Blackley is to support people to live fulfilled lives through the highest standards of dementia care and specialized facilities, with the belief that dementia should not be a barrier to being part of the community.

Nambucca Heads Uniting Care Ageing and Port Macquarie UnitingCare 'Mingaletta,' were designed by Campbell Luscombe Architects and are facilities serving those with dementia, approximately 90 kilometers apart on the mid-north coast of New South Wales, Australia. Crucial to the design is the owner UnitingCare Ageing's commitment to creating a home-like environment that is deinstitutionalized and fosters a person-centered care approach. This concept is designed as a collection of individual communities within a residential care facility, with small, warm community clusters that have all the features of a home-like environment.

The separate resident wings, largely located on different levels, break down the individual care units into "houses," each with 16 to 20 residents. Each house has its own legible "front door" and entry, and its own kitchen is reinforced by a strong linear hierarchy of privacy, from front door to bedroom and a collection of additional small sitting/lounge areas, which further break down the effect of the shortened corridors.

The architectural design of the building is in harmony with the surrounding natural environment and offers a stylish, spacious lifestyle. It was anticipated that the view from the rooftop recreation terraces of 'Pacifica' to the scenic surrounding hills would offer residents a relaxing, secure outdoor entertaining area. The community at the Port Macquarie site 'Mingaletta' accommodates 110 new single bed/ensuite resident rooms. The 'Mingaletta' site was relatively flat, but being bordered by a highway on one side and a major arterial road on the other, traffic noise was an issue and the site was at some distance from Port Macquarie town center. The design utilized the wings resulting from the care model to create calm landscaped interior courtyards.

Outside the residential "houses," there are resident community spaces: therapy and consulting rooms, a hairdressing salon, library, chapel, and café, to encourage the residents to leave their "house" and create the sense of an outing.

Air Force Villages, Inc.

San Antonio, Texas, USA

Air Force Villages, Inc. / Perkins Eastman

Project type Multi-Level Care/
Continuing Care Retirement
Communities

Site location Urban

Site size 40 acres

Building footprint 3,900m²

Building area 15,735m²

Total building cost US$50.3million

Building cost US$3,186/m²

Date completed June 2011

Photography Casey Dunn

Owner's Statement

Air Force Villages initiated a repositioning of its two self-contained campuses: one location offering an urban lifestyle; the other, a rural setting. The strategic planning focused on addressing future marketability of housing options, as well as amenities for residents. It was crucial that this planning address resident preferences at each campus, while not duplicating options and amenities. Air Force Villages also wished to deinstitutionalize their long-term care and replace their existing model of care with a smaller scale, more intimate, residential model. The resulting plan integrated the campuses, allowing each to stand as a neighborhood within a larger combined context of the Air Force Villages' community.

Right The Mission: resident room patios offer direct outdoor access

Opposite top Independent Living villa clusters form neighborhoods

Opposite middle The Mission: offering rehabilitative therapy services and public outpatient use

Opposite bottom The Mission: each household includes an entry with porch

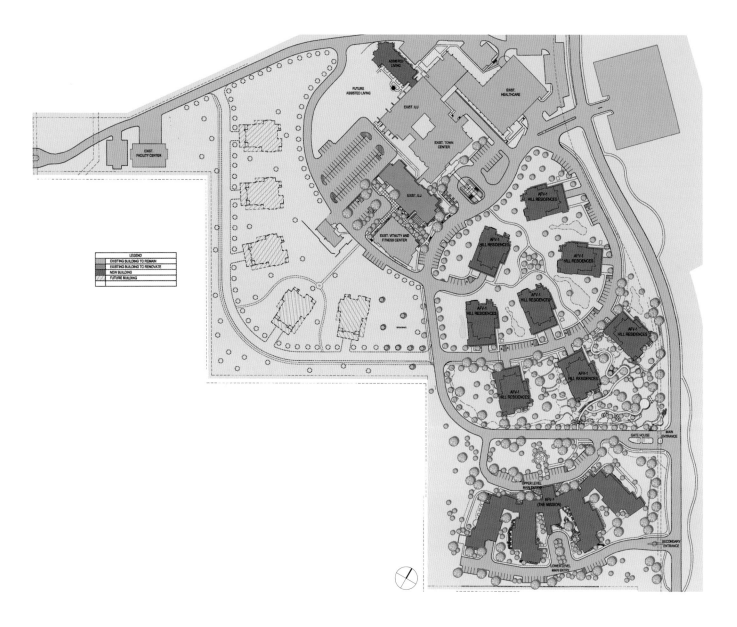

Architect's Statement

The first phase of enhancements included complementing the single large dining venue at each campus with additional options. A new bistro and 16th-floor fine dining sky lounge restaurant and bar were created in the independent living high-rise at Village I. At Village II, a grab-and-go style café revitalizes the existing town center.

Three new four-story independent living Hill Residences were added to the new entry of Village I, replacing existing, smaller duplex-type homes and apartments, which had become less marketable. Village II is adding 75 customized, ranch-style independent living homes, built to suit the residents' lifestyle.

An institutional model of long-term care was replaced with small-scale residential households. Each of the six households centers around a living area with a stone fireplace hearth. This architectural element defines the living room and dining/kitchen area, while maintaining visibility to all resident room entry doors. Each neighborhood features engaging common spaces, including a living room, kitchen, and dining room, with views/connections to landscaped courtyards. The open kitchen and dining rooms allow residents to see, smell, and participate in food preparation. These homelike spaces promote resident gatherings and encourage activities.

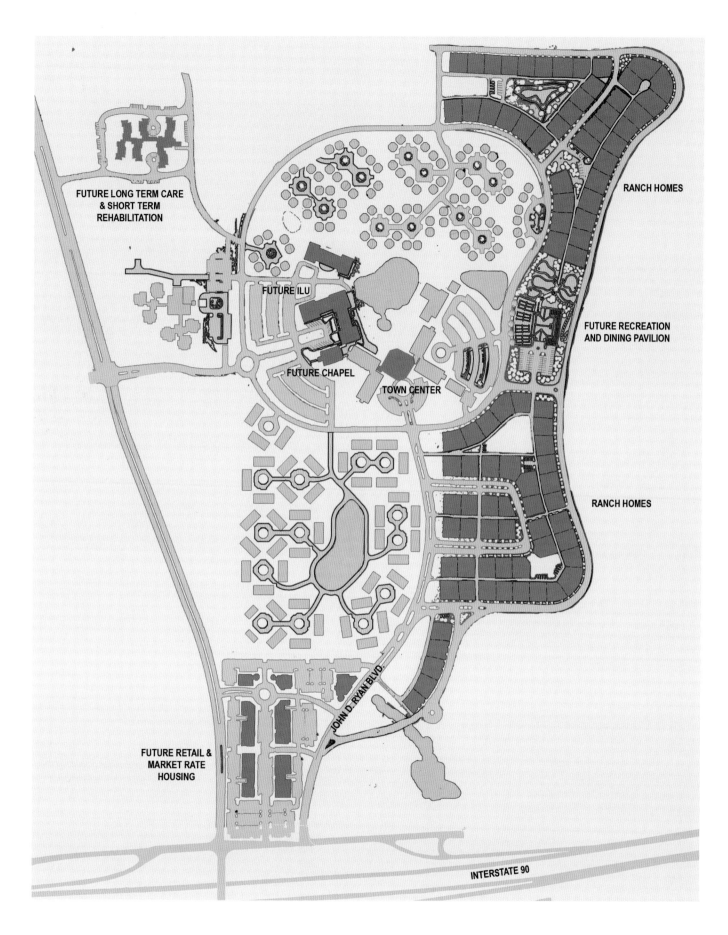

FUTURE LONG TERM CARE
& SHORT TERM
REHABILITATION

RANCH HOMES

FUTURE ILU

FUTURE RECREATION
AND DINING PAVILION

FUTURE CHAPEL

TOWN CENTER

RANCH HOMES

JOHN D. RYAN BLVD.

FUTURE RETAIL &
MARKET RATE
HOUSING

INTERSTATE 90

Opposite Village I Site Plan
Above Village II Site Plan

Client Goals and Design Team Solutions

1 **Client goal:** Repositioning to appeal to the market.

Design team solution: Strategic planning focused on addressing future marketability of housing options and resident amenities. The first phase of enhancements included complementing the large dining venue at each campus with additional options. A new bistro and 16th-floor fine dining lounge/restaurant were created in the independent living high-rise at Village I. At Village II, a grab-and-go style café revitalizes the existing town center. Three four-story independent living residences were added to the new entry of Village I, replacing smaller, less marketable duplex homes and apartments. A small house model of nursing care, which includes provisions for short-term rehabilitation, replaces the existing institutional model. Village II added 75 customized, ranch-style independent living homes built to suit the residents' lifestyle.

2 **Client goal:** Offering choice through a diversity of housing options, including alternative housing.

Design team solution: Three new four-story independent living Hill Residences were added to the new entry of Village I, replacing existing smaller duplex-type homes and apartments, which had become less marketable. A new skilled-care rehabilitation residence, designed in a small house connected model, replaces the existing institutional model. Village II added 75 customized, ranch-style independent living homes built to suit the resident's lifestyle.

3 **Client goal:** Offering daily choice through extensive amenities.

Design team solution: Each campus, previously offering only one large dining venue, gained new dining options. A new bistro and a 16th-floor fine dining sky lounge/ restaurant and bar were created in the independent living high-rise at Village I. At Village II, a grab-and-go style café revitalizes the existing town center.

Major Design Objectives and/or Project Challenges and the Related Responses

1 **A new skilled care/rehabilitation residence:** The owner wanted a small house model of care in one large building, providing residential care and scale, while maximizing efficiencies of shared support spaces and staffing circulation. The team designed a hybrid small house model of six connected households. The massing and building elevations allowed for a unique identity for each household and assisted in reducing overall building scale.

2 **Topography:** Site design took advantage of the challenging, sloping topography and nestled new buildings into the hillside. For the Mission, sloping topography allowed

for two short-term rehabilitation households on the lower level with a public entry; the two households have their own direct entries and private patios off the rooms. The upper level has a main resident and guest entry, and each of the long-term households has its own direct entry; every two households have a private patio. The Hill Residences maximize the topography slide into the hillside, providing an opportunity to have more ground floor units and enclosed parking.

3 **Adaptive reuse:** The design transformed an underutilized multipurpose room and non-marketable ground-floor apartments into a destination sky lounge/restaurant and casual bistro to supplement the campus's existing dining option. Renovating the top floor of the existing high-rise and the ground floor into new dining venues was complex, requiring additional floor space, a new kitchen on the ground floor, and finishing kitchen on the 16th floor, and a new elevator to supplement existing slower elevators. The sky lounge design capitalizes on views and provides a unique private dining venue overlooking the downtown skyline. The bistro energizes the building's base.

Top The Mission: main reception interiors say "home"
Opposite top The Mission: resident room plans
Opposite bottom The Mission: resident rooms include full private bathrooms and patio

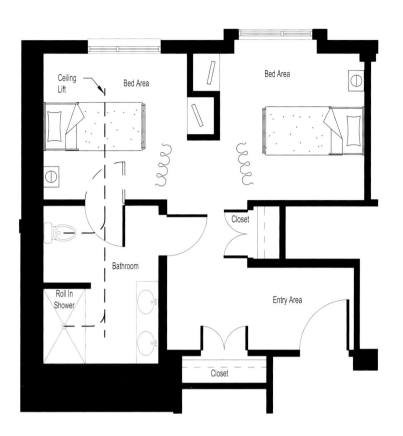

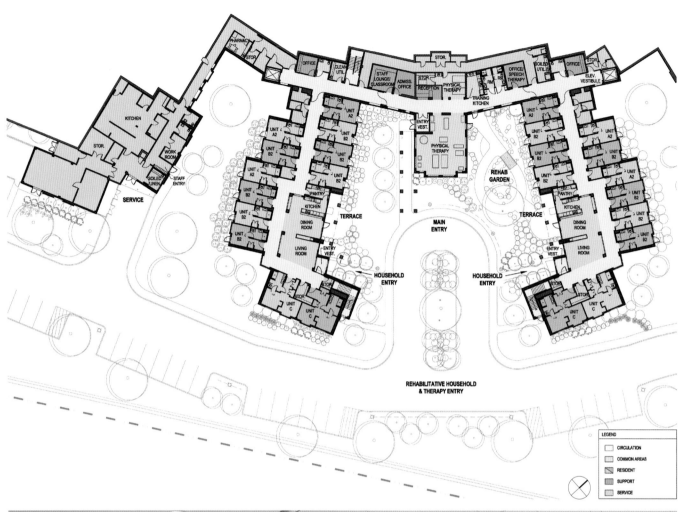

18

Unique Context

The master plan addresses two distinct campuses, viewing each as a unique entity, while part of a greater neighborhood, addressing resident preferences at each campus without completely duplicating options and amenities. At Village I, an underutilized multi-purpose room atop the high-rise apartment building offered the perfect opportunity to create a unique dining destination for residents of both campuses to enjoy—the Sky Lounge restaurant and piano bar.

Because Village II had an abundance of land, the ranch homes seem a perfect fit—built to suit those who like living in detached homes. At Village I, the compact site lent itself to the multi-story Hill Residences. This provided two distinct housing options for prospective residents at each campus.

Existing cottage homes at Village I had become less marketable because of their smaller size, outdated amenities, and aesthetic. However, the site area would not allow a one-for-one replacement with a similar, updated product. The Hill Residences were developed as a new option to satisfy the consumer. Ten-to-fourteen-unit buildings created an intimate, new residential option. All corner units with updated amenities provide an intermediate scale on the campus. In the small house, skilled care and rehabilitation residence, care was taken to individualize the households, creating six separate homes. Each has a distinct name, entry, front porch, and outdoor space.

Environmental Sustainability & Energy Conservation

Sustainable elements include:

- Development on existing, already developed site

- Adaptive reuse of existing spaces

- Low-maintenance, native landscaping

- Progressive water management

- Centralized water and air systems

- Earth-sheltered design*

- Daylighting and views for residents and wayfinding connectivity

*The earth-sheltered design of the Mission reduces energy use. Strong slopes on a portion of the site allowed the building to be set into the earth, allowing the back-end corridors and service rooms at the lower level to be earth-sheltered. A significant part of the exterior envelope of the building is now naturally protected from the sun, lowering energy loads and balancing temperatures with the earth banks.

Advanced Technology

Resident security and safety were important to the client. In the Mission, state-of-the-art technologies that optimize care and safety support aging-in-place. A non-intrusive nurse call system uses profiles to track resident habits and alert staff when behavior differs from usual patterns. Wandering settings can be customized to provide each resident with the maximum level of freedom compatible with their safety. Each unit has the capacity to be equipped with ceiling lifts, improving resident and staff wellbeing.

Design & Philosophy of Care

Air Force Villages wished to deinstitutionalize their long-term care and replace their existing institutional model with a smaller-scale, more intimate, residential model. The new skilled care/rehabilitation residence is designed in a small house connected model and contains six distinct households. It was important that each household created a smaller identity for residents to call home. Each household also has a separate entry from the outside, breaking down the scale of the building.

Integration of Residents with the Broader Community

As a military retirement community, extra attention has been paid to security. However, the Mission was designed with a distinct entry for rehabilitative therapy services, welcoming outpatient users in while also maintaining comfort and security for long-term care residents and their visitors. Additionally, future phases planned for each campus earmarked land in front of the campuses that can be used for mixed-use, intergenerational lifestyle centers.

Opposite top The Mission: lower level floor plan
Opposite bottom The Mission: small-scale, residential household living

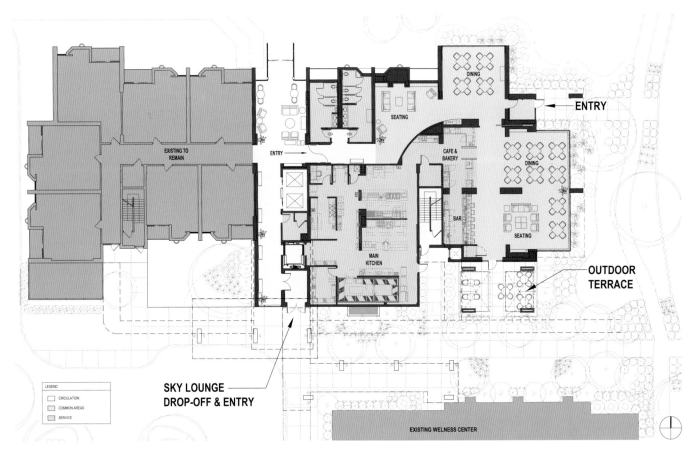

EXISTING TO REMAIN

ENTRY

ENTRY →

DINING

SEATING

CAFE & BAKERY

DINING

BAR

MAIN KITCHEN

SEATING

OUTDOOR TERRACE

SKY LOUNGE DROP-OFF & ENTRY

LEGEND
CIRCULATION
COMMON AREAS
SERVICE

EXISTING WELNESS CENTER

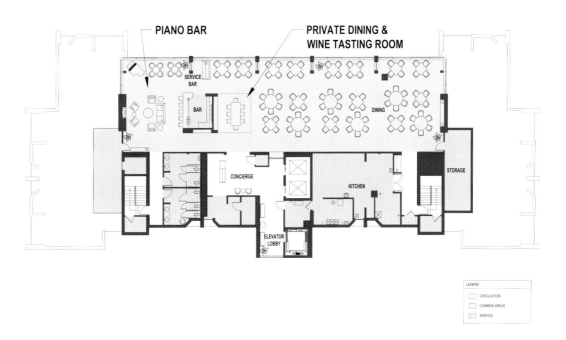

Opposite top Town Center: Cochran's, a casual bistro dining option

Opposite bottom Cochran's bistro floor plan

Top Town Center: destination dining and piano bar

Above Sky Lounge and piano bar floor plan

Above Town Center: heart of Village II features café, computer lounge, library, and activity areas
Opposite Town Center entry lobby at Village II floor plan

Staffing

Total number of staff at this project/facility 575

Number of management staff 78

Number of care staff (registered nursing and direct care staff) 224

Direct care hours per day per client 7.4

Number of other staff (e.g. maintenance, housekeeping, food services) 125

Project Capacity and Number of Units

Independent living cottages/villas 36

Skilled nursing care (beds) 44

Short-term rehab beds 24

Breakdown of Independent Living Units

One bedroom units 3
Typical size per unit 85m^2

Two bedroom units 27
Typical size per unit 107-130m^2

Two bedroom+ units 6
Typical size per unit 142m^2

Breakdown of Skilled Nursing Care Units

One bed/single occupancy rooms 36
Typical size per unit 26m^2

Two bed/double occupancy rooms 8
Typical size per unit 43m^2

Resident/Client Age

Current average age approximately 86 years old

Average age upon entry 82 years old

Resident/Client Fees and Funding

Entry fee Yes

Client Monthly Funding Private (out-of-pocket) pay

Air Force Villages believes that it is possible to match employees' knowledge and skills to resident care needs in a manner that optimizes job satisfaction and care quality. The owner strives for its employee base to ensure quality day-to-day retirement living, with an emphasis on wellbeing. The owner expects its managers to staff adequately and develop employees who are sensitive to the specific emotional needs of the residents.

The non-profit Air Force Village retirement communities include Air Force Village I, which opened in 1970 and is home to more than 500 retired career officers. Air Force Village II, seven miles away, has grown to a vibrant community of 700 residents since opening in 1987. As a Continuing Care Retirement Community, Air Force Village brings peace of mind to residents with facilities and services that include independent living, assisted living, a new standard in skilled nursing and rehabilitation at The Mission, home health, and exceptional Alzheimer's and dementia care at the world-renowned Freedom House.

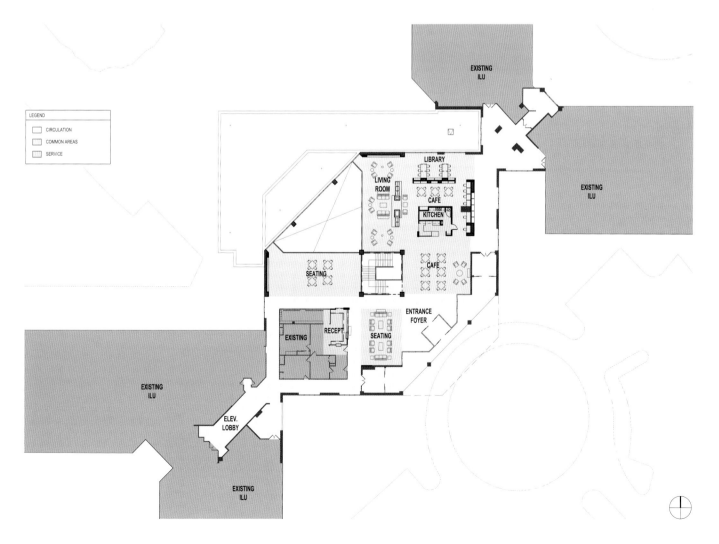

Belong Wigan Community Village

Wigan, Greater Manchester, United Kingdom
Belong / Pozzoni

Project type Active Senior/
Independent Living Residence,
Subsidized Affordable Independent
Living, Special Care Residence
(for those with dementia), Skilled
Nursing Care Residence

Site location Urban

Site size 0.98 hectares

Building footprint 2,845m²

Building area 5,743m²

Total building cost £9,487,858

Building cost £1,652/m²

Date completed May 2011

Photography James White
Photography

Owner's Statement

Belong is a lifestyle concept for older people that aims to prevent isolation and to protect, promote, and uphold a person's autonomy and independence. Belong Wigan Community Village is a two-phased development that incorporates innovative design concepts and details, and is the result of an evolving briefing and design process. Phase one of the scheme was a 66-bed care home and was featured at the IAHSA Design for Aging event in London in 2009. Phase two has seen the completion of 54 independent living apartments and completes the Village.

Belong Wigan Community Village provides 11 private en-suite rooms located within six small, self-contained, open plan, contemporary households that provide individuals with support and rehabilitation opportunities, 24 hours a day. Each house is safe and secure, with access to a garden or balcony. The 54 Independent Living apartments allow for an independent lifestyle within easy reach of the full facilities the community offers.

These environments are where life revolves around purposeful activity and each day has meaning. Belong is a place where life happens, people have fun, and individuals have made an active choice to live in the village. Every day is different and not governed by tasks and time constraints. Opportunities are created for the older person to give care and support to others, as well as receive.

Right Courtyard garden area with community facilities to the right

Opposite top Independent Living Apartments and courtyard

Opposite bottom Rear of care households with bay windows angled to maximize sunlight

Below Ground floor plan: care households and community facilities

Bottom Typical floor plan: Independent Living apartments

Opposite 3D computer view of the Care Village

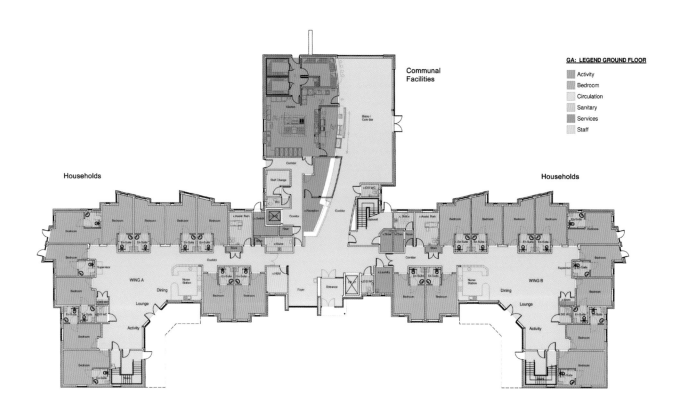

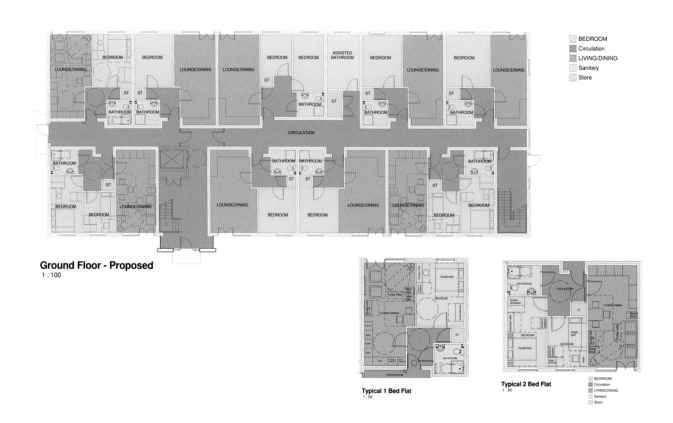

Ground Floor - Proposed
1 : 100

Typical 1 Bed Flat
1 : 50

Typical 2 Bed Flat
1 : 50

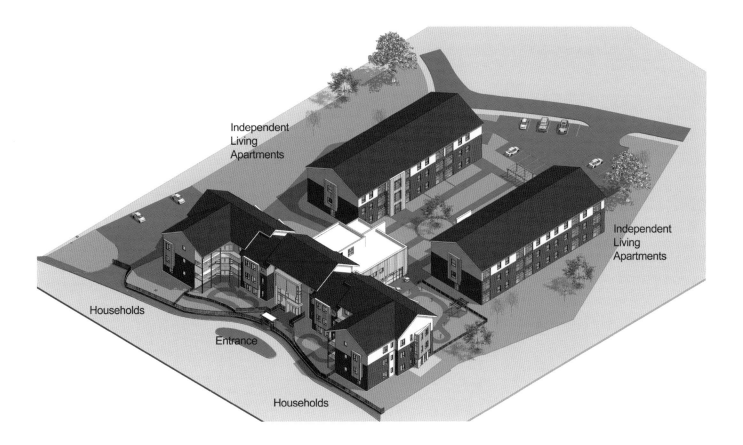

Independent Living Apartments

Independent Living Apartments

Households

Entrance

Households

Architect's Statement

Creating a homely, non-institutional environment is achieved with six self-contained households of 11 residents each, enabling the lifestyle of an 'extended family' to be realized: A domestic, human scale to spaces, details, fixtures, and fittings creates a homely feeling. Each household has its own kitchen, lounge, dining, and activity areas in an open plan configuration so residents can find their way around easily and staff can discreetly monitor residents. Some residents report feeling safer because they can see staff around—in previous homes some people could feel as if they had been left alone if staff were not seen. The 54 Independent Living apartments are also domestic in nature, to maximize independence with easy access to the communal facilities.

Flexible design: For both the Care and Independent Living areas, the floor areas and communal space areas exceed the required standards so the additional floor area allows for large personal possessions and for any additional equipment that may be required in the future. The layout of the en-suite bedrooms allows for future combining of two bedrooms to create a single one-bedroom apartment in the future, should this be required. Dementia design principles have been used throughout.

Community facilities open to the public both within the home and the wider neighborhood: The central 'hub' provides a bistro, hair and beauty salon, community room, visiting doctor room, gym, and internet café. These are designed and fitted out as if they were an independent business, again reinforcing the non-institutional theme. These spaces allow for contact between residents, families, and the wider neighborhood. Several residents, their daughters and grand-daughters may all be having their hair and nails done at the same time, with accompanying gossip and laughter!

Achieving the above while balancing cost and staff issues: Staff enjoy an excellent working environment, incorporating technology to enable them to spend quality time with residents and their families. Staff multi-task and spend their day with the residents, living and working as a large family. Best value has been achieved with the use of thorough value engineering during the procurement process.

Client Goals and Design Team Solutions

1 Client goal: To provide a contemporary living experience for an ageing client group where people feel secure and experience a sense of belonging.

Design team solution: People are helped to live a lifestyle that is familiar, comfortable, and safe with home and family involvement. A change of address need not be a change of lifestyle. Therapeutic activity is valued, companionship with pets encouraged, and intergenerational activity promoted within the community.

2 Client goal: To create smaller living environments that meet the intimate, private needs of individuals, while providing larger spaces to accommodate the more public needs of the community.

Design team solution: There is an increasing need to support the person with dementia through the provision of specialist services within familiar environments, while providing facilities that will meet the needs of the more physically frail person. Villagers will have access to health care specialists without needing to leave the building.

3 Client goal: To create environments where life revolves around purposeful activity and each day has meaning.

Design team solution: Belong is a place where life happens, people have fun, and individuals have made an active choice to live in the village. Every day is different and not governed by tasks and time constraints. Opportunities will be created for the older person to give care and support to others, as well as receive.

Major Design Objectives and/or Project Challenges and the Related Responses

1 Open plan living in safety: The concept of open plan living areas is a departure from conventional thinking about fire safety. The lessons learnt from the previous Belong villages have been incorporated and confirmed that the building design and the management of the fire evacuation strategy are interlinked.

2 Maximizing the potential of the site area without over-development: The economics of high land values and building costs required a high-density scheme. Creating several three-story buildings on the site achieves an economic solution, while retaining the client's key aspirations.

3 Independent living: To reinforce the idea of Independent Living, these apartments are in two blocks—each block has its own front door. Residents and visitors can come and go without passing through a central reception area. Security is maintained with secure access points to the village, intercom entry, and natural surveillance from overlooking windows.

Below Activity in 'The Venue'
community room

Bottom Typical care bedroom
(en-suite shower room to the right,
out of frame)

Opposite Garden areas with points of
activity, outdoor terrace from Bistro
and playground for visiting children

Unique Context

In the UK, government policy is to encourage people to remain in their own homes for as long as possible. Consequently when people do move to a care environment their requirements for care are usually quite high. The principles of designing for people with dementia and other cognitive or physical impairments have been used throughout to accommodate these needs, while also creating a domestic, homely environment. The UK National Dementia Strategy and the 'Prime Minister's Challenge on Dementia' are focusing on dementia as an increasingly priority for healthcare.

The scarcity of sites and high land values require a high-density scheme to work financially. High-density schemes are likely to be more commonplace as land values increase. Belong Wigan has been built on a combination of the location of an existing, outdated, care home plus acquiring several parcels of unbuilt land. The Independent Living apartments provide the option for people to maintain an independent lifestyle, while having specific care packages to suit individual needs.

Building regulations in the UK would normally require fire risk areas to be enclosed behind fire resistant construction. A fire-engineered approach to the open plan households has utilized the combination of a fire-suppression system, compartmentation and a robust fire evacuation strategy to satisfy this legislation.

Environmental Sustainability & Energy Conservation

Thermal modelling during the design phase allowed for a detailed energy appraisal of the design. Energy demand has been reduced with high levels of floor, wall, and roof thermal insulation, zoned heating controls are individual to each room, and all the light fittings and appliances are low energy. Solar shading from balconies and roofs prevent glare and overheating. Local building materials (from sustainable sources) and local tradesmen contribute to reducing the embodied energy in transport.

Advanced Technology

The Belong Village scheme is fitted with a care home nurse call system that covers all 66 bedrooms and community areas. Each bedroom has a specialist dementia network that provides:

- Automatic light guidance for en suite and bed head;
- 16 behaviour profiles;
- Notification of falls or sickness;
- Bed exit sensor and en-suite activity;
- Server that recalls all nurse call activity;

- 24-hour emergency response from the Independent Living apartments.

Each room has a call unit that uses speech, call lead, and pull cord for individual users' requirements. Residents make calls through a call button or neck pendant. There are up to 29 radiofrequency sensors for inactivity, falls, and other alerts, which are included in the individual life plan. All calls go to a DECT phone carried by staff, which has cascade programming for security. Doors are monitored via the panel for security purposes.

Design & Philosophy of Care

The physical layout of the households is simple, orientating, and understandable, to maximize independence. Personal cues such as colour-coding and memorabilia help individuals to identify each room. Décor and furnishing are homely and welcoming, with minimal use of patterns that may cause confusion.

Bedrooms are visible and accessible from the lounge areas. There are private facilities for people who have physical or sensory disabilities. An open and accessible kitchen is central to the household to enable residents to participate in daily living skills. Support is taken to the person, rather than the person to the support, thereby reducing the need for a room or house move as a person's physical condition deteriorates.

Integration of Residents with the Broader Community

Belong has an intergenerational approach and welcomes the local community to use the village facilities.

The Bistro is conveniently situated on the ground floor by the main entrance and has a street presence, welcoming people to take meals and refreshments throughout the day. Themed events are run by volunteers and staff to provide opportunities to socialize.

The hair and beauty salon provides services to residents, staff, and visitors and welcomes the local community. By employing their own salon staff in this bright and contemporary salon, the owner has true team commitment and a feeling of ownership.

The village centre is available for groups such as the Alzheimer's café, Slimmer's world, Steps to Health, to use for functions and entertainment. Cinema evenings are hosted for the local community and dance events. The gym suite is available for older people to use, with the aim of improving wellbeing, and is supported by the local health improvement initiatives.

Top Care household kitchenette
Bottom Bistro, open to the general public

Staffing

Total number of staff at this project/facility 146

Number of management staff 4

Number of care staff (registered nursing and direct care staff) 111

Direct care hours per day per client 2.7 care, 1.35 nursing (as assessed)

Number of other staff (e.g. maintenance, housekeeping, food services) 35

Project Capacity and Numbers of Units

Independent living apartments 54

Special care for persons with dementia 67

Skilled nursing care (beds) 67 (same beds)

Kitchen (daily meals served) 66 meals from 6 household kitchens. Main kitchen serves the main bistro seven days a week

Elder day care (clients) 10

Elder outreach (clients) 38

Fitness/rehab/wellness (daily visits) 12

Breakdown of Independent Living Units

One-bedroom units 35

Typical size per unit 50-53m²

Two bedroom units 19

Typical size per unit 61-71m²

Breakdown of Dementia Special Care Units

Studio/bed-sit units 66, and 1 guest room

Typical size per unit 18-23m²

Breakdown of Skilled Nursing Care Units

One bed/single occupancy rooms 66, as above

Resident/Client Age

Current average age 84 years old

Age upon entry 55 years old

Resident/Client Fees and Funding

Entry fee or unit purchase no

Client monthly funding Private (out-of-pocket) pay

Public/Government funded

Public/Government Subsidies (means tested based on assets and/or income)

Belong's aim is to provide older people with a 'Home for Life' that provides nursing care when needed, until the end of life. Funding will change through reassessment. Residents in the households pay privately or are publicly funded through Local Authority fees. Nursing care is paid for in part or in total by the National Health Service (NHS). The owner charges supplementary payments where fees fall short of the fee required. The current mix is 49 per cent wholly publicly funded for personal or nursing care, 21 per cent part public/private, and 30 per cent wholly privately funded. There are currently 20 people renting apartments. The domiciliary service 'Belong at Home' is paid privately or with direct payments.

Belong is a great place to live and work. The staff put the customer first and their actions are informed by them. People are actively engaged in working in partnership with customers to improve services and identify new service development needs. In doing so, people take personal responsibility for their continuing professional development and support others to use and develop their talents to enhance the customer experience.

Belong staff live the brand and externally they are perceived as 'experts' and 'champions' for the older person. The owner's strategy is to "develop a highly motivated, skilled, and customer focused workforce."

Opposite Front entrance with safe garden area to the foreground

Left Residents enjoying the garden

Cohen-Rosen House

Rockville, Maryland, USA
Charles E. Smith Life Communities / THW Design

Project type Special Care
Residence (for those with dementia)
Site location Suburban
Site size 0.8 hectares
Building footprint 1,520m²
Total building cost US$5.3million
Building cost US$3,488/m²
Date completed October 2012
Photography Alain Jaramillo

Owner's Statement

Building upon the premise of Charles E. Smith Life Communities/Cohen-Rosen House is the leader and provider of choice in delivering innovative services; the design of this environment is based on the layering of the resident's life stories. Incorporating Judaic traditions and historical continuity can be part of making the house a home. The idea is to shed new light upon the resident through a spectrum of daily life activities that will connect them to each other, their families, as well as their caregivers. The common areas of the home are to be portrayed in an open plan, which not only provides residents easy accessibility, but connectivity through socialization. The shared spaces will then become a reflection of their faith, knowledge, history, and their present lives. The intention is to make the resident feel at home by enjoying their family legacies, whether it is through the display of Judaic tapestries, Judaism's most important text—the Torah—Shabbat candlesticks representing the weekly day of rest, or through music.

Above Arrival view
Opposite top Main view
Opposite bottom Main entry

Architect's Statement

At Cohen-Rosen House, wellness begins with the dignity of the resident as reflected through the use of a non-institutional design approach and space relationships that encourage interaction and connectivity with others and with nature. Specific items include the therapeutic nature of the exterior courtyard with water features, gardening tables, and paths and amenities to encourage outside activities. The design of the house encourages interaction with others during daily activities and routines because of the informal open common areas that all residents will use.

The central living room and dining facility will be the heartbeat of the house every day. Artwork is installed throughout and the large art room promotes both physical and mental activities, and will also provide opportunities to interact and work together on projects and activities that promote creativity and conversation. Activities in the dining area, kitchen, and the adjacent library/parlor are intended to also help residents by continuing to do some "normal" tasks as part of their daily routines. There is no institutional space for the caregivers, so their interaction with the residents will be less formal and intimidating to the resident and encourage better relationships and communication. LEED Silver has been achieved so the residents will also enjoy the health benefits of sustainable design. The design team comprised Eric Krull and Jim Hudgins.

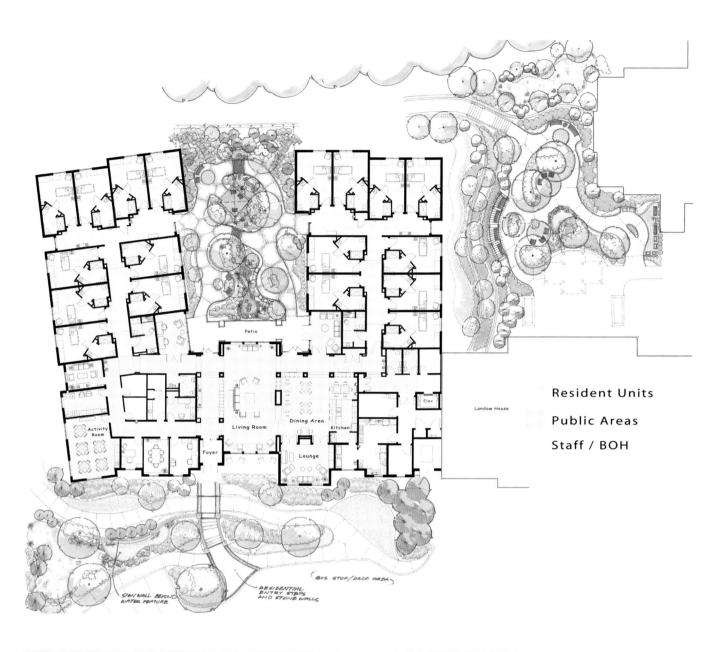

Resident Units

Public Areas

Staff / BOH

Opposite Central living room

Above Site plan

Right Resident room entry with memory box

Client Goals and Design Team Solutions

1 Client goal: Enhanced quality of life.

Design team solution: The quality and connectivity of the spaces, the relationships between the interior and exterior, the design of the individual resident rooms and large memory boxes, the generous use of artwork, and the home-like feel all contribute to an enhanced quality of life. The large centralized living space is bound by a window wall and a front porch on the front and a window wall view of the heavily landscaped resident courtyard at the rear, with an aquarium to one side and open bookshelves and a two-sided fireplace on the other side. The fireplace opens into the dining area, which includes an open kitchen space where the residents can bake cookies or make lemonade with the help of staff.

2 Client goal: Promote wellness.

Design team solution: At Cohen-Rosen House, wellness begins with the dignity of the resident, as reflected through the use of a non-institutional design approach and space relationships that encourage interaction and connectivity with others and with nature. Specific items include the therapeutic nature of the exterior courtyard with water features, gardening tables, and paths and amenities to encourage outside activities. Artwork is installed throughout and the large art room promotes both physical and mental activities. Activities in the dining area, kitchen and the adjacent library/parlor are intended to also help residents by continuing to do some "normal" tasks as part of their daily routines. LEED Silver has been achieved, so the residents will also enjoy the healthy benefits of sustainable design.

3 Client goal: Empower independence.

Design team solution: Each resident has an individual room and a large individual memory box that can reflect their unique situation or personality. As a resident of a large "house," a resident can wander and visit other residents, or sit quietly and enjoy a little personal time in the four-season porch or the quiet room or the library/parlor –thus the resident has options during the day of where to go and what to do. The exterior courtyard is designed to allow residents to use independently of a caregiver, whether the resident wants to walk around and explore or sit and enjoy the view of the trees and listen to the birds singing.

Major Design Objectives and/or Project Challenges and the Related Responses

1 Making a Memory Support unit feel like home: Making an 18-bed Memory Support unit feel like home was a challenging design task. The solution was to design Cohen-Rosen House with spaces you find in your typical home. To accomplish this, the house was broken down into three principal zones: public, private, and back of house. Throughout the interior common areas, the use of residentially scaled materials, finishes, artwork, integrated furnishings, and accessories, gives Cohen-Rosen House the character and feel of a large house, not an institutional facility. The central living room space is the heart of the Cohen-Rosen House. The living room space provides the residents with a "hearth" and a place to anchor themselves everyday, no matter their condition, and makes Cohen-Rosen House a home.

2 Overcoming challenging site lines: There were challenging site lines from adjacent courtyards, and taller existing buildings. To find a resolution, attention was given to green roof solutions, clerestory roof expressions, and creative mechanical equipment enclosures.

3 Creating visual cues of home: Another challenge was creating visual cues within the design, to stimulate and capture the overall feeling of home. The design solution incorporated views to the outdoor courtyards, tree area, and pond. In addition, unique art niches are located at the end of corridors, and memory boxes are outside each resident's room where they can display items that are unique to their personality, family, and life story.

Opposite top Art room
Opposite bottom Gallery with view to exterior gardens

Unique Context

Most often, memory support facilities are designed to keep residents from wandering around freely, but this is not the case at Cohen-Rosen House. It was designed to empower independence. Being residents of a large "house," a resident can wander and visit with other residents, or sit quietly and enjoy a little personal time in the four-season porch or the quiet room or the library/parlor—thus the resident has options during the day or where to go and what to do. The exterior courtyard is designed to allow residents to use independently of a caregiver, whether the resident wants to walk around and explore or sit and enjoy the view of the trees and listen to the birds singing.

Environmental Sustainability & Energy Conservation

Design features used that support environmental sustainability and energy conservation are the Green Roof solutions, clerestory roof expressions and creative mechanical equipment enclosures. LEED certification is being pursued.

Design & Philosophy of Care

At Cohen-Rosen House, wellness begins with the dignity of the resident, as reflected through the use of a non-institutional design approach and space relationships that encourage interaction and connectivity with others and with nature. Specific items include the therapeutic nature of the exterior courtyard with water features, gardening tables, and paths and amenities to encourage outside activities. Artwork is installed throughout and the large art room promotes both physical and metal activities. Activities in the dining area, kitchen and the adjacent library/parlor are intended to also help residents by continuing to do some "normal" tasks as part of their daily routines.

Integration of Residents with the Broader Community

Cohen-Rosen House is a new addition to the Charles E. Smith Life Communities, a campus of Jewish services in Montgomery County, Maryland. It is co-located with a skilled nursing facility, independent living, and assisted living for seniors. It shares the campus with the elementary grades of a Jewish Day School, a synagogue pre-school, the athletic center and programming at the Jewish Community Center, an Adult Day Center, and a Jewish Social Services Agency. Cross-generational and inter-agency programming benefits all. Programming routinely brings the community into the facilities and rich activities take residents to outside programming, shopping, and events.

Above Living room with view to dining

Staffing

Total number of staff at this project/facility 24

Number of management staff 2

Number of care staff (registered nursing and direct care staff) 16

Direct care hours per day per client 5.88

Number of other staff (e.g. maintenance, housekeeping, food services) 6

Project Capacity and Numbers of Units

Special care for persons with dementia 18

Breakdown of Dementia Special Care Units

One bedroom units 18
Typical size per unit 360m²

Resident/Client Age

Current average age 88 years old

Average age upon entry 88 years old

Resident/Client Fees and Funding

Entry fee or unit purchase no

Client monthly funding Private (out-of-pocket) pay

Cohen-Rosen is a small, memory care assisted living service that complements the senior services on campus. More than 1,100 seniors call the campus home. This new residence is private pay and balances the mix on the entire campus. On the campus, more than 65 per cent of the residents are Medicaid or subsidized. Cohen-Rosen House allows the project owner, Charles E. Smith Life Communities, to fulfill its mission.

Cohen Rosen House utilizes the universal worker concept. Everyone is trained to care for individuals with Alzheimer's disease and dementia. Every staff member assists with activities of daily living, housekeeping, recreation, and dining. Here, everyone is universal. Each staff member is specifically trained to assist residents with whatever they need, when they need it. At Cohen-Rosen House, the Geriatric Nursing Assistant is a "Life Skills Partner." Staff consists of a Manager, a LPN on each shift, Life Skills Partner, two Activity Assistants, and a light and heavy duty Housekeeping Technician.

Opposite top Dining room
Opposite bottom Computer lounge
Above Resident room

EachStep Blackley

Blackley, Manchester, UK
Community Integrated Care / Pozzoni

Project type Community-Based
Services, Special Care Residence
(for those with dementia), Skilled
Care Nursing Residence

Site location Urban

Site size 0.4 hectares

Building footprint 1,260m²

Building area 3,764m²

Total building cost £4,056,506

Building cost £1,652/m²

Date completed June 2012

Photography James White
Photography

Owner's Statement

EachStep Blackley is a pioneering, £5million dementia service based in Manchester, UK, which offers a complete range of support for people with dementia—home care, day care, respite care, and residential and nursing care. By providing this holistic package of support from one central service, the owner and provider, Community Integrated Care, is in the unique position of being able to support people with dementia each step of the way, in their own homes and in their specialist service.

EachStep Blackley is a vibrant service where people are supported to be happy, engaged, and well cared for. The provider supports the mental stimulation and physical wellbeing of people who access their service, ensuring that they remain part of their communities and follow the interests and activities they enjoy.

With their highly trained staff, specialist facilities and philosophy of always supporting people to enjoy happy and fulfilled lives, EachStep Blackley offers the highest standards of dementia care. They believe that dementia should not be a barrier to being part of the community. Because of this belief, they support people to still be part of local life and encourage members of the community to be part of the service.

Right EachStep front view from
main road

Opposite top Courtyard garden

Opposite bottom Site plan

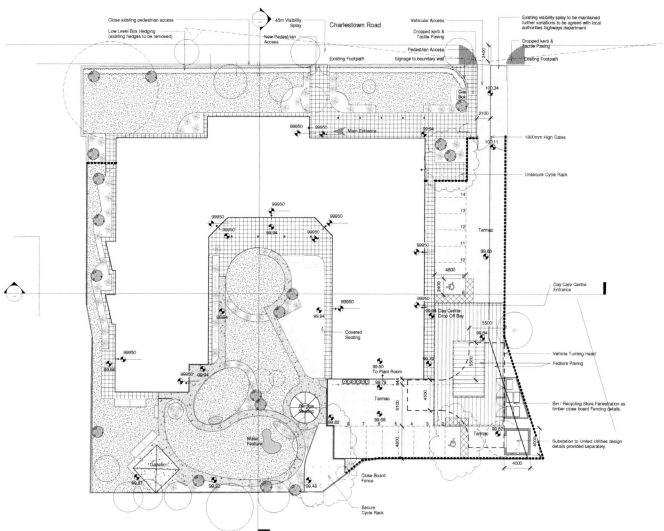

Close existing pedestrian access
45m Visibility Splay
Charlestown Road
Vehicular Access
Existing visibility splay to be maintained further variations to be agreed with local authorities highways department

Low Level Box Hedging (existing hedges to be removed)
New Pedestrian Access
Dropped kerb & Tactile Paving
Dropped kerb & Tactile Paving

Existing Footpath
Pedestrian Access
Signage to boundary wall
Existing Footpath

Gas Box

100.34

2100

99950   99950   Main Entrance   99.94
1800mm High Gates

100.11

1800mm High Gates

Unsecure Cycle Rack

14
13
12
Tarmac

99950   99.88
11
10
4800   9
2400   8

99950
Day Care Centre Entrance

99.98
Day Centre Drop Off Bay
5500

99.64
99.94   99950

99950
Covered Seating

99.94
99.70
5500

99950

Vehicle Turning Head
Feature Paving

99.60
To Plant Room   99.79

Pergola Seating
99.69   644
4800   6100

Tarmac

Bin / Recycling Store Fenestration as timber close board Fencing details.

99.82   99.69
6
5

99.62

Water Feature

4800   4

Tarmac   Substation to United Utilities design details provided separately.

Gazebo   3   2   1

4000

99.27
99.23
Close Board Fence
99.46

4000

Secure Cycle Rack

45

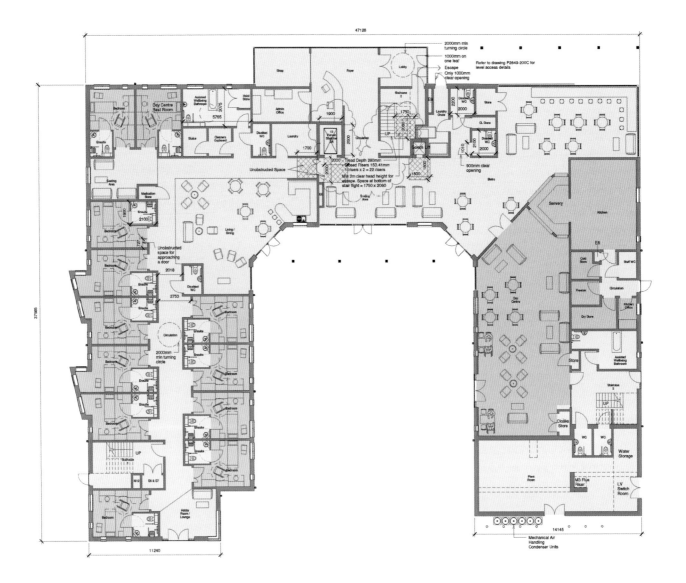

Architect's Statement

Four households of 12 residents are self-contained, with their own kitchen, lounge, dining, and activity areas in an open plan configuration. This contributes to the domestic lifestyle with a human scale to spaces, details, fixtures, and fittings. The open plan allows residents to easily orientate themselves and for staff to keep a discreet eye on them. The fifth household offers respite care.

There are facilities for the use of the community within the home and the wider neighborhood. There is a coffee shop open to the wider community and this is the first dementia care facility in the UK to have a 'Costa Coffee' franchise. This provides the opportunity for contact between residents, families, and the wider neighborhood. The community resource is also enhanced by basing the EachStep homecare service here and the provision of both day care and respite care within the building.

Designing in the flexibility for current and future use creates a 'Home for Life': Older people have and will continue to have a higher expectation of design and

service. The floor areas and communal space areas exceed the national minimum standards. Larger floor areas allow space for residents' personal possessions to be brought in if they wish and for additional equipment to be used, should a resident's needs change. The principles of designing for people with dementia have been adopted throughout the design.

Balancing staffing and cost issues: An excellent environment has been created for the staff, with the use of assistive technology enabling them to spend more quality time with residents. The open plan design allows staff to carry out their roles in an efficient and non-institutional way. Value engineering sessions throughout the design and construction process have eliminated waste and promoted best value.

Client Goals and Design Team Solutions

1 **Client goal:** EachStep Blackley offers specialist residential and nursing care that is focused on enabling people with dementia to live happier, more independent, lives.

Design team solution: The bespoke, state-of-the-art service and specially trained staff offer the very best in dementia care. The households have been custom-designed to promote the independence, safety, and wellbeing of people with dementia, applying the latest innovation and research in dementia care, yet still feel homely and welcoming.

2 **Client goal:** Respite care offers people with dementia short-term residential care and support. This support can be invaluable, giving family and other carers a well-deserved break, or helping people with dementia who are unable to continue living in their own home for a short period of time.

Design team solution: EachStep Blackley includes a large respite household, which supports up to 12 people. Based on the ground floor, as per the design of the other EachStep households, it includes a range of specialist facilities to support independent living and give residents the very best in respite care.

3 **Client goal:** A large, spacious specialist dementia day care service can accommodate up to 25 people at a time and has been specially designed to be accessible for people with dementia, and offers a wide range of activities to fulfill every member's interests. Dementia can makes it difficult to stay in contact with friends, pursue hobbies, and meet new people.

Design team solution: Day care is a great way to remain active, meet and make friends, have fun, provide mental stimulation, social interaction, and support for staying independent for longer. Dementia day care can also help family or other carers, allowing them to take some time out of their caring routine.

Major Design Objectives and/or Project Challenges and the Related Responses

1 The concept of open plan living areas is a departure from conventional thinking about fire safety. A fire engineered approach including a fire suppression system, building compartmentation, and a robust management strategy which combine to create an environment beneficial to people with dementia, without compromising safety.

2 Maximizing the use of the site. Building costs and the relatively high value of land requires small sites to be of a high-density. The design process arrived at a mostly three-storey building as achieving an economic solution, while retaining the goals and objectives.

3 Access to external space is essential. The respite care and day care areas have direct access to garden spaces, and while the residential and nursing care households on the upper floors can still access the gardens via the stairs/lifts, the upper floor households have a shared balcony. There is much debate about the suitability of balconies for people with dementia. A higher than conventional handrail, visual access for staff to the balcony, and individual risk assessments for residents ensure ease of access with safety.

Opposite Floor plan
Left Courtyard garden

Unique Context

The UK government encourages people to remain in their own homes for as long as practical and feasible. Consequently, when people do move to a care home, they are more likely to have higher dependency requirements. The principles of designing for people with dementia and other cognitive or physical impairments have been used throughout to accommodate these needs, but avoiding an institutional environment. The UK also has a National Dementia Strategy and the 'Prime Minister's Challenge on Dementia,' with dementia becoming an increasingly priority for healthcare.

A lack of suitable development sites coupled with high land values require care developments to be of a high density, in order to work financially. These high-density schemes are likely to be more commonplace as land values increase. EachStep was built on the site of an outdated care home, which was in the client's ownership.

Conventional design to accommodate UK building regulations would require fire risk areas to be enclosed behind fire resistant construction. The open plan households have been created with a fire-suppression system, compartmentation, and a robust fire evacuation strategy.

Environmental Sustainability & Energy Conservation

A dynamic thermal model was produced, allowing for an in-depth energy appraisal of the building design. High levels of thermal insulation, low energy light fittings and appliances and individual room heating controls reduce the demand for energy. Balcony and roof overhangs prevent glare and overheating. Where possible, building materials have been sourced locally and local tradesmen have been used, reducing the embodied energy in transport. Building materials have been obtained from sustainable sources.

Advanced Technology

Lights in communal areas, storerooms, and toilets switch off when that area is unoccupied. Also, in each bedroom next to the bathroom door, adjacent to the bed, lights illuminate the way to the bathroom when a resident gets out of bed.

MyAmego® is a person-centred system enabling users to maintain quality of life and a degree of 'independence' without constant intrusive monitoring by carers. It gives service users and carers confidence that risks to individuals are being monitored and alerted.

The BeMAR wireless scanner is an electronic monitored dosage medication system with paperless MAR chart. It is synched to the iPad, so domiciliary carers, nurses and care home staff scan Biodose pods during their rounds. My Life Software™

has developed Digital Reminiscence Therapy Software™, an innovative software solution providing communication support and interactivity for the elderly and people with dementia.

Design & Philosophy of Care

The physical layout of the households is simple, orientating, and understandable, to maximize independence. The open plan households are divided up into distinct lounge, dining, and activity areas. Décor and furnishing are homely and welcoming.

There are no dead ends, which can be confusing for people with dementia. An alcove sitting area at the end of each corridor creates an 'event.' An open and accessible kitchen is central to the household, to enable residents to participate in daily living skills.

Large windows, low windowsills, angled bay windows, and building orientation maximize natural daylight and ventilation and promote general wellbeing among residents and staff.

Integration of Residents with the Broader Community

The coffee shop is situated on the ground floor with a street presence, welcoming people throughout the day. Open to the public, the café becomes a meeting place for residents, their families, and the wider public, promoting social interaction and breaking the stigma and barriers often associated with care facilities.

Respite care offers people with dementia short-term residential care and support. This support can be invaluable, giving family and other carers a well-deserved break, or helping people with dementia who are unable to continue living in their own home for a short period of time. EachStep Blackley includes a large respite household, which supports up to 12 people. Based on the ground floor, as per the other EachStep households, it includes a range of specialist facilities to support independent living and give residents the very best in respite care.

Daycare can accommodate up to 25 people at a time and has been specially designed to be accessible for people with dementia and offers a wide range of activities to fulfill every member's interests. Dementia can makes it difficult to stay in contact with friends, pursue hobbies, and meet new people. Day care is a great way to remain active, meet and make friends, have fun, provide mental stimulation, social interaction and support for staying independent for longer. Dementia day care can also help family or other carers, allowing them to take some time out of their caring routine.

The service ensures that the people it supports are able to access the community, for instance supporting many people to visit local shops and other such amenities. It also provides regular opportunities for residents to enjoy stimulating days out—offering daytrips to a mix of places that will be familiar to them, as well as new experiences. EachStep also includes internet facilities, enabling many residents to keep in touch with their family and friends, and stay up-to-date with news from their local community, online.

Above Typical care bedroom (en-suite shower room not shown)
Right Kitchenette

Staffing

Total number of staff at this project/facility 90

Number of management staff 3

Number of care staff (registered nursing and direct care staff) 77

Direct care hours per day per client 5

Number of other staff (e.g. maintenance, housekeeping, food services) 13

Project Capacity and Numbers of Units

Special care for persons with dementia 60

Skilled nursing care (beds) 24, plus 36 residential/respite beds

Kitchen (daily meals served) 60, plus coffee shop

Elder day care (clients) 25

Breakdown of Dementia Special Care Units

Studio/bed-sit units 60

Typical size per unit 18-23m²

Breakdown of Skilled Nursing Care Units

One bed/single occupancy room 60

Typical size per unit 18-23m²

Opposite top Daycare room

Opposite bottom Living area

Below Coffee shop at prominent corner of the site

Resident/Client Age

Current average age late 70s/early 80s

Average age upon entry Over 50 years old

Resident/Client Fees and Funding

Entry fee or unit purchase no

Client Monthly Funding Private (out-of-pocket) pay

Public/Government funded

Public/Government Subsidies (means tested based on assets and/or income)

58 per cent of residents get funding from the local authority and pay a 'top up' fee. 29 per cent of residents are private payers and 13 per cent of residents receive 'Continuing Health Care' funding for their high dependency needs. Wherever possible, people are supported by a consistent staff team. This helps the staff build strong relationships with the people they support, and gives people consistency and familiarity in their care.

Staff get to know the people they support—their interests, life history, likes, and dislikes, to offer each person a bespoke package of support. To make life easier for people with dementia and their family carers, EachStep offers a complete range of dementia support.

Everyone working for EachStep receives specialist dementia training to understand the condition, its complexities and how best to support people with the condition. Dementia should not be a barrier to being part of the community. Because of this belief, EachStep supports people to still be part of local life and encourages members of the community to be part of their service.

EnsenCare Tianning
Senior Living Community

Changzhou, China

**EnsenCare, a member of Legend Holdings China /
THW Design, USA / Origin Architect, China**

Project type Multi-Level Care/
Continuing Care Retirement
Communities

Site location Urban

Site Size 33,000m²

Building footprint 10,000m²

Building area 87,000m²

Total building cost US$80 million

Building cost US$970/m²

Date completed anticipated
December 2014

Photography courtesy of the
architect

Owner's Statement

The owners were looking to be at the forefront of a creative solution to address the serious and social economic challenge that faces China's growing senior population. Facing the culture challenge to provide a continuum of care community for seniors in China, the team created a unique solution by reinventing the Continuing Care Retirement Communities (CCRC) model to meet the local market demands and by incorporating a Senior College and gerontology-focused hospital that also serve the broader community. By offering integrated social services to the community at large, the project was deemed *for the greater good of all*, which is highly regarded by the government. The aging-in-place concept was very important to the client from the beginning. They did not want residents to be forced to move from their home as their care needs increased. The reinvented CCRC model would minimize independent living focus and emphasize multi-generational living by incorporating active adult apartments; this will support the Chinese culture by offering solutions for families to live together and have access to personalized care for their elders in their declining years.

Above Community view from canal

Opposite top Skilled Nursing living/dining area

Opposite bottom Aerial view

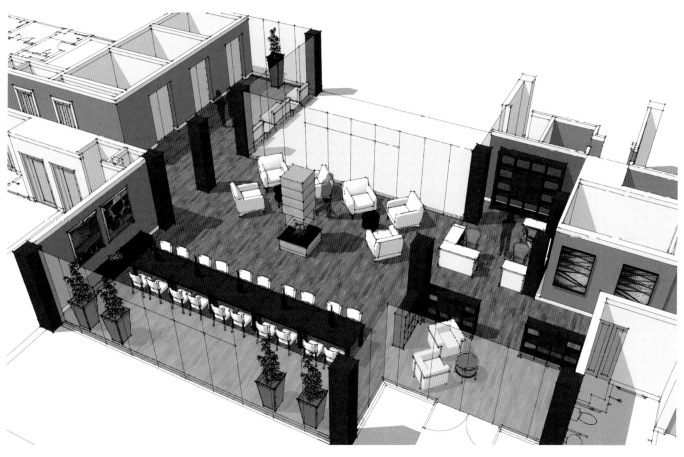

MULTI-GENERATION
ACTIVE ADULT HOME

EXISTING CANAL

ASSISTED LIVING
HOME

NURSING HOME

CLUBHOUSE

SENIOR COLLEGE

HOSPITAL

SENIOR COLLEGE

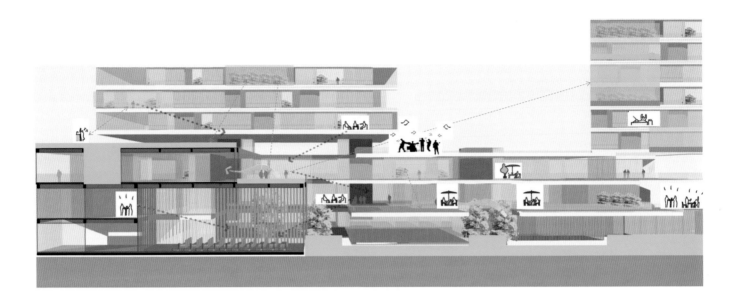

Architect's Statement

The goal is to meet the challenges of designing a community for the rapidly aging population in China, one providing new homes embodying a healing and vital lifestyle. This relevant and unique program establishes high-value objectives that include strategically locating the Senior College to be the central focus for a united community of varying levels of care and integrating residents with the broader community, supporting multi-generational culture and providing a social energy focus.

The universal design of the different levels of care provides flexibility from the beginning. Residents will not be forced to move from home, as their care needs increase and the building design remains flexible to adjust to the changing market, Assisted Living and Skilled Nursing can be easily converted, allowing residents to age in place. For example, not only will the Skilled Nursing offer nurse

care stations, but Assisted Living homes will also offer fully staffed care stations, where residents have access to immediate care.

It is important to distinguish the community from the militaristic rows of high rises and provide a wellness-based design that encourages activity and participation by residents, as well as interaction with the outside community that reinstates purpose for the lives of residents.

The design provides a green environment that feels comfortably inviting and non-institutional. It encourages indoor–outdoor integration to keep residents from the loneliness of their room, and softens the hard edges that typical urban high rises have in order to create a more natural environment that is a uniquely landscaped urban community for retirement. The design team comprised Song Cheng, Mark Tilden and Ji Li.

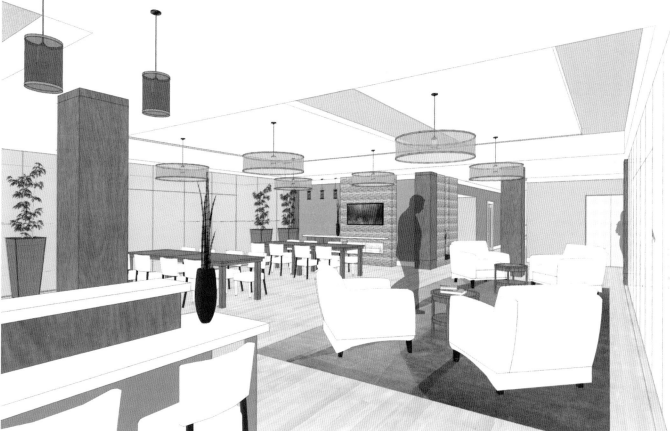

Opposite Vertical analysis for green design
Top Lobby view
Above View from care station

Client Goals and Design Team Solutions

1 Client goal: Provide a high-quality planned community choice for China's aging demographic.

Design team solution: The owner's staff has been researching the world's solutions and they toured example campuses in many countries around the world. Their goal is to learn from designers about the best solutions and provide their own combination of ideas to create a community for China's aging population that will endure.

The solution combines high efficiencies of Japanese concepts with many of the benefits of social confluence planning designed in the best CCRC campuses in the USA. The designers provided tours and the owner/operator/architect team collaboratively found the solution with all levels of care in an active healthy community design.

2 Client goal: Provide a campus that serves the aging community by keeping their life active and integrated with the community rather than isolating the senior residents.

Design team solution: By opening the campus to the community, the residents interact with all ages and sustain a life of purpose serving the young and the old through volunteer programs, integrated learning opportunities, and dining/activities that can be private or intergenerational. The solution incorporates some private secure program club functions for residents only. Other areas in the program such as the college and clinic, invite public participation, expanding senior residents' opportunities to stay part of the larger community, serving as teachers, students, and participants.

3 Client goal: The client wants to teach the public about the new ways of care for their aging population. Change is difficult; by serving the varying needs of the community and teaching the public about what is offered, the acceptance of a new solution for care will take hold for a culture that already seeks ways to care for aging people; and China's 5-Year-Plan requires it.

Design team solution: The Senior College is designed with seven centers of learning geared for seniors but also open to the public. This "Win-Win" strategy not only educates the public, but also markets the campus. The seven centers are: Health, Education, Cooking, Painting and Art, Calligraphy, Dance, Foreign Languages, and Skills & Fitness. Retail shops along the public streets also attract public attention to the campus.

Major Design Objectives and/or Project Challenges and the Related Responses

1 Encouraging activity and relaxation: How can the design setting and configuration encourage activity and relaxation, thereby creating more opportunity for socialization and general wellness fulfillment? Service functions are kept below ground and awareness of any delivery or staff activity is kept to a minimum. An active central landscaped courtyard is the focus of active indoor spaces in the Independent Living and Assisted Living areas, Skilled Nursing, College, Clinic and Office surrounds. Resident rooms are mostly south-facing and oriented to overlook the courtyard.

Platforms of landscaping- indoor and outdoor surround the courtyard for easy horizontal circulation at all levels. This encourages walking and engaging in activities. It allows for synergy and flexibility of activities that can be appreciated by the whole group (concerts, parties, visiting children, competitions, etc.).

2 Making one unified community: The urban site is divided by an existing river, yet needs to be one unified community. Active adults participating in the community broaden the market. The architect planned the Active Adult section of the campus to the north side of the river just outside the heart of the campus. Many of this age group still work and are more transient, but appreciate concierge living and convenient high-quality care. The south campus design includes a clubhouse with wellness and restaurant choices for all to share. Long- and short-term care are both provided in a non-institutional setting. Amenities align the river and pedestrian links provide easy access to the central campus courtyard. The site solution focuses attention from all levels of living experience to a shared active landscaped courtyard. This synergized view focus creates a relaxed atmosphere. Active Adult Community residents can enter the courtyard for activity and then transverse the river to return to their neighborhood, but are still an integrated part of the designed community.

3 Providing security for residents: How do you get the social benefit of inviting the public to actively enjoy your campus, but at the same time provide security for the residents? The college, office, and clinic are shared by the public and secured in a traditional way. The clubhouse is operated like a private country club with membership required, but certain meals are open to participants in the college and clinic programs. Skilled Nursing and rehab function with highest security and have more privacy and access control. Gates to the community are limited and outside service is kept to basement levels or monitored/scheduled by staff.

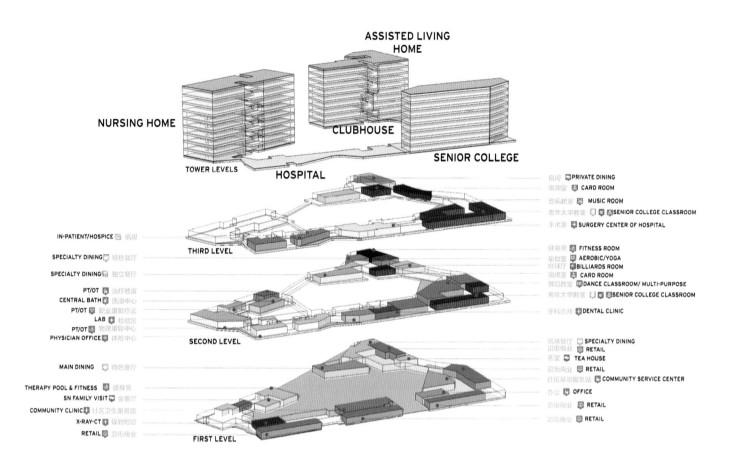

ASSISTED LIVING
HOME

NURSING HOME

CLUBHOUSE

SENIOR COLLEGE

TOWER LEVELS

HOSPITAL

THIRD LEVEL

包间 🔲 PRIVATE DINING
棋牌室 🔲 CARD ROOM
音乐教室 🎵 MUSIC ROOM
老年大学教室 🔲 🔲 SENIOR COLLEGE CLASSROOM
手术室 🔲 SURGERY CENTER OF HOSPITAL

IN-PATIENT/HOSPICE 🛏 病房

SPECIALTY DINING 🔲 特色餐厅
SPECIALTY DINING 🔲 独立餐厅
PT/OT 🔲 治疗教室
CENTRAL BATH 🔲 洗澡中心
PT/OT 🔲 职业康复疗法
LAB 🔲 检验区
PT/OT 🔲 物理康复中心
PHYSICIAN OFFICE 🔲 体检中心

SECOND LEVEL

健身房 🔲 FITNESS ROOM
瑜创室 🔲 AEROBIC/YOGA
台球厅 🔲 BILLIARDS ROOM
棋牌室 🔲 CARD ROOM
舞蹈教室 🔲 DANCE CLASSROOM/ MULTI-PURPOSE
老年大学教室 🔲 🔲 SENIOR COLLEGE CLASSROOM
牙科诊所 🔲 DENTAL CLINIC

MAIN DINING 🔲 特色餐厅

THERAPY POOL & FITNESS 🔲 健身房
SN FAMILY VISIT 🔲 会客厅
COMMUNITY CLINIC 🔲 社区卫生服务站
X-RAY-CT 🔲 放射检验
RETAIL 🔲 沿街商业

FIRST LEVEL

风味餐厅 🔲 SPECIALTY DINING
沿街商业 🔲 RETAIL
茶室 🔲 TEA HOUSE
沿街商业 🔲 RETAIL
社区基层服务站 🔲 COMMUNITY SERVICE CENTER
办公 🔲 OFFICE
沿街商业 🔲 RETAIL
沿街商业 🔲 RETAIL

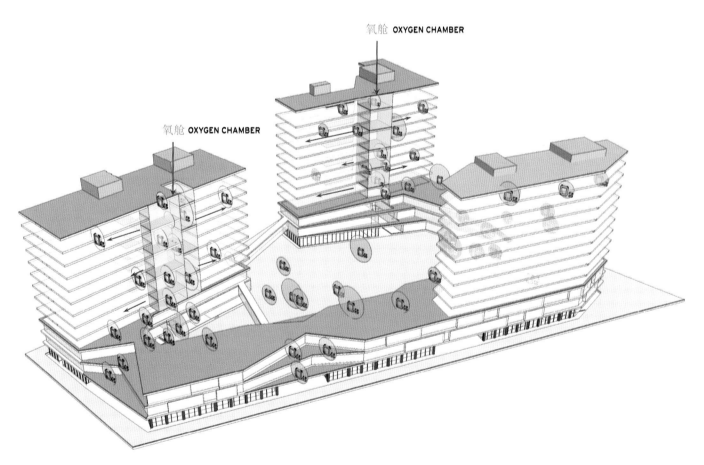

氧舱 OXYGEN CHAMBER

氧舱 OXYGEN CHAMBER

Top 3-dimensional plan analysis
Above Patio/balcony and open space analysis

Unique Context

The Chinese culture values multi-generational living, with 90 per cent of China's seniors currently living at home under the care of their families. These families have very few options when it comes to continued care or community that focuses on the changing healthcare needs of their parents and grandparents. The new community will meet these needs as an intergenerational senior-focused community. By re-inventing the CCRC model to replace Independent Living with an Active Adult Community, this will support the Chinese culture by offering solutions for families to live together and be able to care for their elderly members in their declining years.

Environmental Sustainability & Energy Conservation

Project design features that support environmental sustainability and energy conservation include:

- Orientation of building to utilize natural light and ventilation to reduce air conditioning cost;

- Green roof garden reduces urban heat island effect, and reduces energy cost;

- Solar energy collector for hot water use;

- Extra insulation for walls saves 25 per cent, compared with traditional construction and energy-efficient windows.

Advanced Technology

Project design considerations that take into account the programme's intention to utilize advanced technologies for operations and/or resident care include:

- Electronic medical records systems;

- Two-way nurse call system;

- Motion detection in resident rooms for safety;

- State-of-the-art fitness equipment in the PT/OT rehab

Integration of Residents with the Broader Community

Project design and/or programme elements that support the integration of elder residents with the broader community include:

- The college with seven centers of learning for seniors will serve the aging public, as well as the residents of this community. Students have controlled access to meals in the clubhouse restaurants;

- The clinic and rehab (PT/OT) are open to public use;

- Street-front retail shops are shared with the public;

- The government office building includes a public service center that will increase public awareness of the campus; this large space is positioned at a primary intersection of the site. Once a visitor is inside the government center, the view opens out to the central active courtyard and its surrounding activities, which makes the public aware of the amenities offered by the community.

Staffing

Total number of staff at this project/facility 237

Number of management staff 23

Number of care staff (registered nursing and direct care staff) 160

Number of other staff (e.g. maintenance, housekeeping, food services) 100

Project Capacity and Numbers of Units

Independent living apartments 263

Assisted living/hostel care 156

Skilled nursing care (beds) 186

Breakdown of Independent Living Units (combining both apartments and cottages/villas)

One bedroom units 200
Typical size per unit 60m²

Two bedroom units 63
Typical size per unit 100m²

Breakdown of Assisted Living/Hostel Care Units

One bedroom units 130

Typical size per unit 50m²

Two bedroom units 26

Typical size per unit 70m²

Breakdown of Skilled Nursing Care Units

One bed/single occupancy rooms 186

Typical size per unit 50m²

Resident/Client Age

Current average age 55 years old+ (target)

Resident/Client Fees and Funding

Entry fee or unit purchase Yes

Client monthly funding Private (out-of-pocket) pay

The general population of China's seniors is approximately 60 per cent female, 40 per cent male, and the community is projected to reflect a similar ratio.

Opposite Landscape analysis
Below Plan diagram

轮椅出行半径

| 200m | 100m | 30m | 0m |
| 需要协助 | 自理较为吃力 | 可以轻松自理 | |

HammondCare Miranda

Sydney, New South Wales (NSW), Australia
HammondCare / Allen Jack + Cottier

Project type Special Care Residence (for those with dementia), Skilled Nursing Care Residence

Site location Suburban

Site size 49,000m² (including proposed Independent Living development – still in Master Planning phase)

Building footprint 6,220m² (including eight cottages, administration building, and chapel/amenities block)

Building area 6,220m²

Total building cost AUS$26 million

Building cost AUS$4,180/m²

Date completed December 2012

Photography Allen Jack + Cottier (Nic Bailey)

Owner's Statement

Hammond Care is passionate about improving the lives of older people living with dementia. To put this into practice, HammondCare Miranda is distinctly different from most skilled nursing facilities in Australia. It is designed to be a real home separated into eight small cottages with all the elements of home life—kitchen, laundry, living room, and garden. Four of the cottages have 15 single bedrooms, while the other four have just eight single bedrooms (extremely unusual in the Australian context), which are well suited to a more personalized model of care.

The small-scale cottages have been designed to be flexible enough to reflect and accommodate the personality and life history of each resident. The domestic environment within each cottage allows for natural encounters between staff and residents and activities, such as cooking, cleaning, and washing, reflecting the rhythms of normal home life.

Although it is difficult to find appropriate and affordable parcels of land in suburban Sydney, each of HammondCare Miranda's eight cottages has its own secure garden area with a continuous path, which loops between different external entry/exit doors. This open access to the outdoors is supported by the evidence on good dementia design.

Right Residents in all cottages have access to secure garden areas.

Opposite top Visual access: staff and residents can see bedroom corridors, small lounge areas, and outdoor spaces from the cottage's central hub.

Opposite bottom The central kitchen and living areas of a 15-bed cottage– the pivotal anchor point of the home

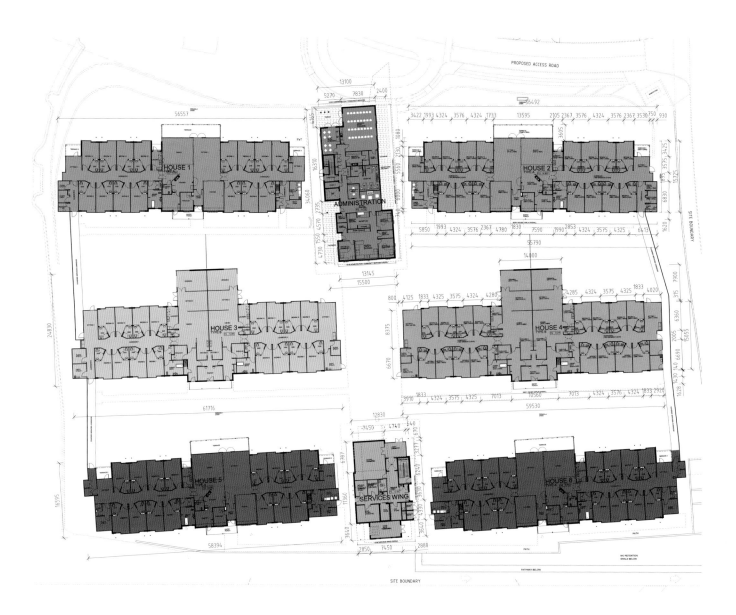

Architect's Statement

The planning and design of HammondCare Miranda is the result of comprehensive research and collaboration between HammondCare and Allen Jack+Cottier Architects. The objectives were to design a distinctive development that would overcome negative preconceptions of seniors living, while creating an environmentally responsible development that would enable 'ageing in place,' while integrating seniors into the broader community. The project provides for a Stage 1 skilled nursing facility (completed) and Stage 2 independent living units with support facilities that can be shared with the broader community (still in Master Planning).

The design philosophy informing the skilled nursing facility was derived from the principle of 'form follows function,' providing a 'prosthetic' built environment that complements care services. The development is overlaid with a sense of place within each house that is distilled from 'home.'

The HammondCare model is best suited to flat sites, but this was not possible at Miranda. Cross fall in excess of 5 meters and a potential of overshadowing along the south-eastern corner of the site presented challenges that were resolved by providing a basement for laundry services, deliveries, and parking. The houses were also stepped across the site (maximum 1:20 gradient), ensuring good universal access while diffusing potential overshadowing issues.

Above HammondCare Miranda site plan
Opposite top An exterior half-elevation of a 15-bed cottage
Opposite bottom An exterior elevation of an eight-bed cottage

LEGEND

Terra cotta roof tile
'Mineral'

Zinc tray roofing
'Graphite Grey'

FC horizontal planking
'Pale parchment' paint finish

Face brick
'Ironstone red homestead'

Timber weatherboard
'Soot' acrylic finish

Timber weatherboard
'Cygnet grey' acrylic finish

External timber
'Soot' acrylic finish

Colorbond
'Woodland grey'

Anodised aluminium
'Satin sandstone'

External doors
'Burning brier' paint finish

Timber entry door
Clear varnish satin

Clear glazing

LEGEND

Terra cotta roof tile
'Savanna'

Zinc tray roofing
'Graphite Grey'

FC horizontal planking
'Fiji sands' paint finish

Face brick
'Central west homestead'

Detail brick
'Ironstone red homestead'

Timber weatherboard
'Soot' acrylic finish

Timber weatherboard
'Cygnet grey' acrylic finish

External timber
'Soot' acrylic finish

Colorbond
'Woodland grey'

Anodised aluminium
'Satin quarry beige'

External doors
'Tibetan silk' paint finish

Timber entry door
Clear varnish satin

Clear glazing

Client Goals and Design Team Solutions

1 Client goal: To create small intentional communities for groups of older residents and staff to focus on living active, vibrant lives. To recognize that within those communities, feeling safe is crucial for people's wellbeing, to recognize the value of feeling in control.

Design team solution: The skilled nursing facility has been designed and built as eight separate single-story cottages facilitating ease of access. To create a sense of identity and security, each home is differentiated in multiple ways, from the color of the roofing tiles, external brickwork, and paints, right down to the door handles on each resident's bedroom door.

2 Client Goal: To promote a calm, home environment free from institutional intrusion.

Design team solution: The design of the eight cottages has incorporated two external 'service corridors' connected to storerooms, clean and dirty utility areas, covered walkways, and concealed 'back of house' entries that allow deliveries of clean linen, food, and supplies, without interrupting residents. The short travel distances and small number of residents in each cottage remove the need for trolleys in the homes. Fully functioning kitchens free the facility from institutional routines, while almost all maintenance can be carried out in the service corridors and 'back of house' areas.

3 Client goal: To establish a central focus in each of the cottages with good visual access.

Design team solution: A conscious decision was made to make the kitchen and living areas a pivotal focal point in each household. The sights, sounds, and smells that are reminiscent of 'home' are connected to the kitchen and living areas and serve as an anchor for spatial organization, readily identifiable throughout the cottage. The bedroom corridors can also be seen from all public living areas, while the garden path, which returns the resident to living areas, is clearly visible from the back door.

Major Design Objectives and/or Project Challenges and the Related Responses

1 Orientation: Not 'knowing' and feeling uncomfortable in an environment results in anxiety and alienation. To address this, the cottages have been designed with no dead ends or blind corridors, resulting in a generally more serene sense of place, which is beneficial to all within the household. Orienting the resident to their room, each bedroom has a 'front door' with differing door handles and scotia molding. Each bedroom door is signposted with a collection of personal memorabilia in a framed window box, capturing who the individual is through key moments and memories from their life.

2 Interior architecture—light and lighting: The brightness and quality of light is an important aspect of the visual environment for supporting older people, particularly those with dementia, who need lighting to be twice as bright as normal interior levels. HammondCare Miranda has more lights with higher wattage than a standard domestic setting, while high ceilings with skylights in the corridors and large windows introduce natural light into the living areas of the cottages. The result is higher levels of light, providing a clearer view of spaces within the home, while minimizing glare.

Right A resident bedroom
Opposite Two of the cottages have roof top solar panels.

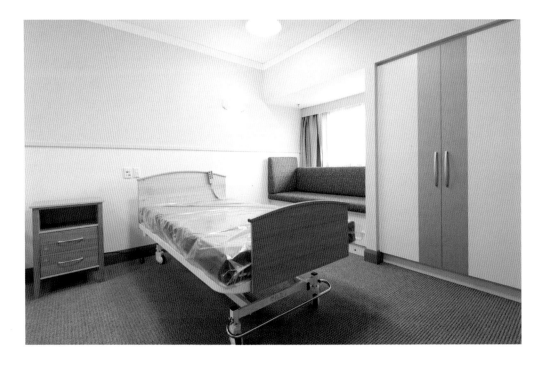

Unique Context

HammondCare Miranda has been built using face bricks and terracotta roofing tiles, both common building materials for homes in the local area. The facility is located in the Sutherland Shire of Sydney, an area defined by water with a strong beach culture. This is reflected in the interior design and landscaping, with 300 photos and artworks depicting well-known local landmarks and coastal, native plantings in the gardens.

Another important facet of home life in suburban Sydney is the backyard space. HammondCare Miranda's outdoor areas have been designed with the key elements of a typical backyard, including lawns, a garden space, and the quintessential 'Hills Hoist' rotary clothesline—clearly visible from each cottage's domestic laundry—adding to the sense of normality.

Single-occupant bedrooms with their own private, ensuite bathrooms are increasingly desired and expected in the Australian aged care market and HammondCare Miranda meets this expectation. The cottages have been designed with a higher quality fit and finish, including upscale light fittings, Corian benchtops in the kitchens and feature walls in all resident bedrooms, while still upholding the principles of good dementia design.

Environmental Sustainability & Energy Conservation

A strong focus has been placed on the use and re-use of both water and electricity at HammondCare Miranda. Each of the cottages is fitted with 1,000-litre capacity rainwater retention tanks and the harvested water is used to irrigate the gardens. The site is also equipped with stormwater detention storage to facilitate the timely removal of excess water. Two of the cottages have photovoltaic cells on their roofs, generating 50kW—10 per cent of the site's electricity needs. These solar panels are used to run a gas-boosted solar hot water system.

Design & Philosophy of Care

HammondCare's philosophy of care is about maximizing independence, freedom of choice, and life engagement. This is supported by:

- Contrasting colors, which highlight important elements in the environment, such as faucets (which contrast with basins) and toilet seats (which are a different color from toilet bowls);

- Concealed doors and a lack of contrast to disguise potential risks such as staff-only areas, fire extinguishers, and dirty utility doors; and

- Consistency of color in indoor and outdoor flooring surfaces, to reduce the risk of falls. This minimizes the negative effects of visual perceptual disorders among people living with dementia.

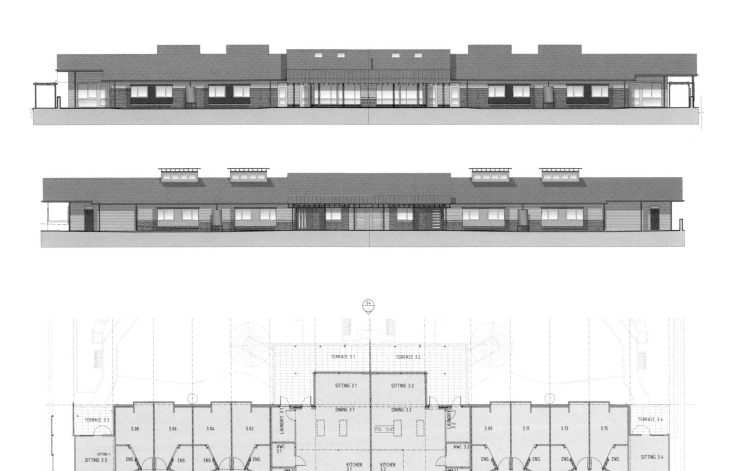

Staffing

Total number of staff at this project/facility Approximately 100*

Number of management staff 4 (1 Operations Manager, 2 Facility Managers and 1 Client Liaison Manager)

Number of care staff (registered nursing and direct care staff) 10 registered nurses and approximately 85 Specialized Dementia Carers

Direct care hours per day per client >3

Number of other staff (e.g. maintenance, housekeeping, food services) 7 (1 Workplace Trainer, 2 Administration Workers, 1 Pastoral Care Coordinator, 1 Maintenance Worker, 1 Respite Program Coordinator and 1 Volunteer Coordinator) plus sessional work from allied health professionals and hairdressers.

The cottages at HammondCare Miranda are primarily staffed by multi-skilled Specialized Dementia Carers (SDCs) who provide face-to-face personal care and assist residents to maintain independence while carrying out domestic duties such as cooking and cleaning. Working alongside the SDCs are registered nurses known as Specialized Dementia Advisors (SDAs). The SDAs support the SDCs by providing clinical oversight, mentoring and advice. For example, while the SDCs give and receive handover at the change of shifts, the SDAs assist by reviewing the handover and providing advice on clinical matters and behavioural issues as appropriate.

*All numbers are estimates based on a full occupancy rate of 92.

Project Capacity and Numbers of Units

Skilled Nursing care (beds) 92

Breakdown of Skilled Nursing Care Units

One bed/single occupancy rooms 92
Typical size per unit 25m² (including ensuite bathroom)

Resident/Client Age

Current average age 83.4 years old

Entry fee Yes

Client monthly funding Private (out-of-pocket) pay

Public/Government Subsidies (means-tested based on assets and/or income)

Resident/Client Fees and Funding

HammondCare Miranda is a dementia-specific, ageing-in-place skilled nursing facility with capacity for 30 low-care and 62 high-care residents. Low care residents and 'Extra Service' high-care residents with sufficient assets pay a periodic accommodation charge or bond to enter the facility. All residents who can afford to pay a basic daily fee, which covers living expenses, while those with sufficient income also pay an income-tested fee. The government subsidizes residents who cannot afford to pay. At least 20 per cent of residents are subsidized by government.

Opposite top Elevation and floor plan of two 8-bed cottages
Opposite bottom A 'cottage' yard with lawn, garden spaces and the quintessential Australian Hills Hoist rotary clothesline
Above A cottage entrance with a distinctive front door and colour scheme

Holy Spirit Boondall

Brisbane, Queensland, Australia
Holy Spirit Care Services / Bickerton Masters Architecture

Project type Multi-Level Care/
Continuing Care Retirement
Communities
Site location Suburban
Site size 4,175 hectares
Building footprint 6,902m²
Building area 25,287m²
Total building cost AUS$52.8 million
Building cost AUS$2,807/m²
Date completed October 2012
Photography Bickerton Masters
Architecture

Owner's Statement

Holy Spirit's aim was to provide a new community-based approach to senior living. Holy Spirit Boondall is a care and lifestyle development for persons over the age of 70 years of age. Its goal is to provide a continuum of care and services from fully independent living through to high-dependency living in a specialist nursing center staffed 24 hours a day, 7 days a week, by professionally trained nursing staff. The development comprises 128 one-, two- and three-bedroom units, secure parking, community facilities, and a 10-room high-care specialist nursing center all contained in a single building.

At the heart of our philosophy and purpose is Holy Spirit's Mission Statement: "To touch and enhance the lives of people through our Christian culture of quality care and service." It continues the mission of the founding congregation, the Holy Spirit Missionary Sisters. The Holy Spirit Boondall community has been developed with Holy Spirit's mission and that legacy at its heart.

The vision for Holy Spirit Boondall is about bringing that mission to life through contributing positively to the lives of those who live there. It is an holistic approach based on Christian values of respect, integrity, compassion, justice, and innovation and delivered with a high-quality standard of care and service.

Holy Spirit Boondall is a landmark development for the Boondall area and for the standard of seniors' living in Brisbane. Its modern contemporary design and careful planning has enabled a high-density development, unique to the area, to blend in successfully with the existing environment.

Right Entry to aged care facility
Opposite top Retirement apartments viewed from the community podium
Opposite bottom Aerial view

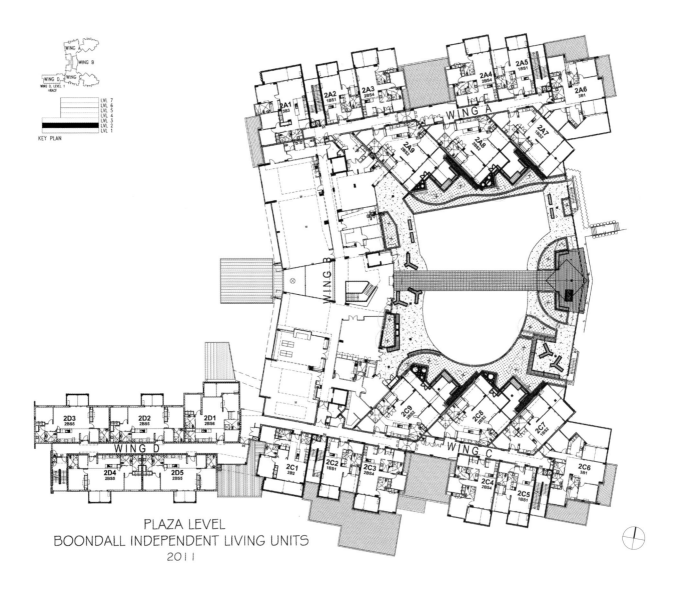

KEY PLAN

PLAZA LEVEL
BOONDALL INDEPENDENT LIVING UNITS
2011

Architect's Statement

Holy Spirit Boondall comprises 128 one-, two-, and three-bedroom apartments, secure car parking, community facilities, and 10 high-care beds all contained within a single building.

To achieve a seven-story outcome in this area, where there is nothing else of this scale, the massing and form of the building had to be carefully modeled to visually reduce the bulk of the residential towers.

There are two residential towers that share a podium that contains community facilities. The towers flank a podium garden deck containing community recreational facilities and providing a social hub for activities.

Each residential tower has its own lobby and there is a central lobby for visitors, staff, and residents that link the ground and first floor community spaces.

The orientation and configuration of the apartments allow most apartments to have views to the north, south, or east over the golf course. Harsh western exposure is minimized.

The towers are linked and high level to provide opportunity for ease of resident access to their neighbors. Residents and carers can travel between towers without traveling more than one floor up or down within the building.

Residents will be able to select their own personal level of engagement with subsets of the community from the groupings of 11 in each tower floor level 'neighborhood,' the whole floor of between 14 and 27 apartments, or the entire community of 128 apartments by partaking in a function in the level 2 function room, meeting up for coffee in the café or doing a little gardening in the community gardens on the podium and around the building.

The building design provides the opportunity for residents to make their own choices about the level of social inclusion with which they feel comfortable.

Above Floor plan
Opposite top View from the golf course
Opposite bottom RACF set-down

Client Goals and Design Team Solutions

1 Client Goal: Achieving a yield in excess of 100 apartments.

Design team solution: Early schemes for the site and initial planning advice indicated a potential yield of around 50 apartments in a maximum four-story building. The site was constrained on all sides with a creek corridor to the south, a golf course to the east, a school to the north, and a road and commercial precinct to the west. To achieve the yield required, the architect needed to produce a multi-story solution in a location where there was no precedent for this. To successfully achieve this outcome, the architects produced extensive 3D modeling of the building to display its context with the surrounding environment. The building itself was carefully modeled to reduce bulk and scale, and façade treatments enhanced this.

2 Client Goal: Enhancing the surrounding environment.

Design team solution: The site is bounded to the south by a creek corridor. The client identified this as a recreational opportunity for residents. The creek corridor also acts as a buffer to light industry activities to the south of the site. A rehabilitation scheme was put in place to remove weeds and inappropriate tree species and replace them with native planting to supplement existing significant vegetation, which has been retained. Bio-retention works are assisting to clean stormwater before it is discharged into the creek. An interpretive boardwalk has been constructed, allowing access to the creek corridor for the elderly and this links into an exercise path that circumnavigates the site.

3 Client Goal: Providing an energy efficient, sustainable design.

Design team solution: The siting and orientation of the building have minimized exposure to the west. Nearly all apartments have north, south, or east-facing aspects, achieving maximum benefit from views over the creek corridor and golf course and minimizing heat load from the west. Rainwater is harvested and stored to provide irrigation for the landscaped grounds.

Major Design Objectives and/or Project Challenges and the Related Responses

1 Building on a site that was previously an underutilized, flood-prone part of a school campus: Detailed flood studies were commissioned to display that the proposal would be both flood-immune itself and also provide a solution that would not create issues for surrounding landowners. The local authority commended the submission for the detail provided in the flood study at planning approval stage. This resulted in a successful outcome on a site previously thought to not be suitable for development. This development has provided an opportunity to address the flooding issues while providing a facility that will be home to more than 200 people, and also a broader destination for the surrounding neighborhood.

2 Providing a safe, secure environment for residents: The building has been organised into two residential towers that are linked at podium level with community facilities. The internal community spaces open out onto a first floor podium deck that provides residents with the opportunity to participate in a variety of active and passive recreational pursuits without the need to leave the building. A secure car park at ground level provides residents with secure access directly to their apartment. Residents can visit friends in the apartment tower via an internal link and receive priority care from nursing staff. Staff security after hours is also a critical factor, and the center has been designed to allow staff to access all areas of the facility without the need to leave the building.

3 Constructing a low-maintenance building: Holy Spirit Care Services will be a long-term owner/operator of this project. It was important to provide them with an easy-to-maintain low recurrent cost building. The architect's solution was to provide a building with low-maintenance façade treatment on higher levels (i.e. aluminum cladding) and limit painted surfaces to low levels, which are easy to access. This provides an opportunity to revitalize the building without the future need for expensive scaffolding.

Opposite top Community centre foyer under construction
Opposite bottom Chapel

Unique Context

The site is on the suburban fringes of Brisbane, a sub-tropical city in Queensland, Australia. The site is on a parcel of land that has been sub-divided from an existing school site. The land is on a floodplain and needed some significant amelioration to make it suitable for this use. The project sets a precedent for a scheme of this height and density in this part of Brisbane.

Environmental Sustainability and Energy Conservation

Rainwater is harvested and stored for irrigation of landscape areas and use in bathrooms of the aged care facility for toilet flushing. The apartments are orientated to minimize western exposure.

Advanced Technology

This is the first multi-story retirement facility in Queensland to have access to the National Broadband Network (NBN). This will provide a unique level of connectivity for the residents.

Design and Philosophy of Care

Holy Spirit's philosophy of care is about contributing positively to the lives of people who live there. The building delivers on this philosophy by providing a safe, secure, and high-quality environment where residents have the opportunity to participate in life in a supportive community to a level with which they feel comfortable.

Integration of Residents with the Broader Community

The residents of the retirement community have forged links with the adjoining school. Students partake in activities in the residents' community facilities, providing benefits for each.

Project Capacity and Numbers of Units

Independent living apartments 128
Skilled nursing care (beds) 10
Kitchen (daily meals served) 100
Fitness/rehab/wellness (daily visits) 30
Pool(s) and related areas (daily visits) 30

Breakdown of Independent Living Units

One bedroom units 8
Typical size per unit 65m^2
Two bedroom units 108
Typical size per unit 95m^2
Two bedroom plus units 18
Typical size per unit 120m^2

Breakdown of Skilled Nursing Care Units

One bed/single occupancy rooms 10
Typical size per unit 21.8m^2, with 5.9m^2 ensuite

Opposite RACF community spaces
Top Bold lines of the apartments
Left Apartments oriented to views and solar access with enhanced privacy
Below Apartments overlook the landscaped community podium.

Holy Spirit Westcourt

Cairns, Queensland, Australia
Holy Spirit Care Services / Bickerton Masters Architecture

Project type Active Senior/
Independent Living Residence

Site location Suburban

Site size 2.7 hectares

Building footprint 2,473m²

Building area 7,310m²

Total building cost AUS$17.7 million

Building cost AUS$2,421/m²

Date completed September 2012

Photography Andrew Watson
Photography care of Hutchinson
Builders (pages 76, 78 and 79);
Bruce Clarke/Clarke and Prince
Architects (pages 77, 81, 82 and 83)
and Bickerton Masters Architecture
(page 80)

Owner's Statement

Holy Spirit Westcourt is a five-stage redevelopment of two adjoining sites—Coral Sea Gardens Retirement Village and Bethlehem Nursing Home—located in the central suburb of Westcourt in Cairns, Queensland.

The architect's vision for the redevelopment of the two sites was to combine them into one community and create a continuum of care approach that reflected Holy Spirit's mission and values, while maintaining the community legacy of Bethlehem Home in Cairns created by the people of Cairns, the Sisters of Mercy, and the Diocese of Cairns in 1972.

The new community facilities such as the café and the chapel are open to the public and the running of other areas such as the gym and hairdresser provide opportunities for local businesses to extend their operations to Holy Spirit Westcourt residents.

In summary, Holy Spirit Westcourt is a landmark development for Catholic healthcare in Cairns and for the standard of seniors' living in Cairns. The modern contemporary design and choice of features and facilities blend both the existing Coral Sea Gardens and Bethlehem Nursing Home communities together to create a vibrant seniors' living complex that successfully embodies the objectives of the Holy Spirit's mission and values.

Right Entry plaza and set-down

Opposite top Bethlehem Nursing Home

Opposite bottom Internal landscaped courtyard, Bethlehem Nursing Home

Architect's statement

Three of the five stages of the master-planned, integrated residential community at Westcourt, Cairns are now complete and contain 86 high care beds, 38 apartments, and shared community facilities.

Stage 1 is a two-story 86-bed residential aged care building. It replaces out-of-date barracks-like accommodation, which was no longer meeting the safety or security needs of the residents, visitors, or staff.

The aim was to create a new home for existing residents, which addressed safety, privacy, security, and care issues, without compromising the sense of community that was already evident on site. The architecture breaks the building down into a fine-grained domestic scale through the use of a variety of façade elements and materials.

The bedrooms are organised into eight 'houses,' linked to a core containing resident living and dining spaces and courtyards. The figure-8 layout provides for staff efficiency and creates internal landscaped courtyards for the residents to access for passive recreation.

Stage 2 provides community facilities for both the RACF and Retirement Apartments. It provides a new front door for the site. The shaded plaza will become the social hub for the site. Various community spaces are accessed from the plaza, including chapel, function room, café, hairdresser, and gym.

In line with its status as the focal point for the site, the community center is designed to be colourful, appealing, and appropriate for its tropical setting. It is designed to draw the wider community into the site.

Stage 3 is a four-story retirement apartment building containing 38 one-, two-, and three-bedroom apartments fronting Gatton Street. The apartments are configured to appear like three separate but linked buildings to maintain a residential scale. The use of a variety of façade materials reinforces this notion. Wide overhangs, deep balconies, screens, and shutters, together with roof forms, contribute to the tropical vernacular. Stages 4 and 5 will complete the streetscape to Gatton and Brown Streets, and the landscape treatment providing the tropical setting for the community facilities.

Above Retirement apartments

Client Goals and Design Team Solutions

1 Client Goal: Addressing security and care issues of the existing facility.

Design team solution: The master-planned integrated community provides a secure environment for elderly residents by providing passive surveillance over street frontages and back into the site from residents' apartments. The pedestrian paths in landscape space between buildings are well lit and provide clear direct access to the front door of each component of the project. The two-story nursing center provides access to all resident community spaces under one roof and incorporates outdoor rooms on each level to provide residents access to secure outdoor shaded spaces. In addition to this, internal landscaped courtyards provide a secure space for residents to access nature.

2 Client Goal: Attracting the broader community to the site.

Design team solution: The central plaza space provides a landmark feature for the site and this space will provide opportunity for social connection. The space links the high care and retirement precincts within the site and also presents a welcoming statement to the wider community through use of color, architectural forms, and activity, to encourage broader local community use of the spaces.

Major Design Objectives and/or Project Challenges and the Related Responses

1 Redevelopment of an existing outdated facility while remaining in operation on the site: The architects produced a staged solution which first replaced the existing aged care beds in a two-story building containing 86 beds, each with a private ensuite, community dining lounge, and activity spaces, and also replacing existing administration facilities. Once residents and staff had been relocated into their new home, this allowed demolition of the existing inappropriate building stock. A central community center and 38 retirement apartments have recently been completed on the site of the old care facility. This development has occurred with minimal disruption to the residential staff.

2 Achieve approval for four-story development in a part of Cairns where previously only two-story was permitted: The client had a desire to yield in excess of 100 apartments on this site. The architect wanted to achieve this and still provide a style of accommodation different to the existing single-story duplex dwellings on the adjoining site. The architect developed a four-story solution that addressed the street frontages and allowed for a large central community green space. The local authority was supportive of this approach and approval was attained.

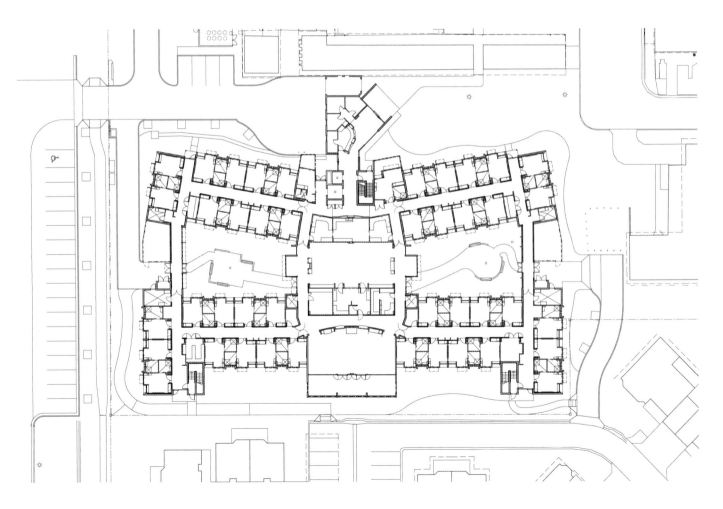

Opposite Floor plan of Bethlehem Nursing Home

Top A courtyard creates an outdoor room

Above left Foyer of Bethlehem Nursing Home

Above right A semi-enclosed verandah space provides opportunity for alfresco dining.

Unique Context

The project is located in Cairns in the tropical north of Australia. Buildings are all designed with wide roof overhangs and awning to windows to provide protection from the sun. Buildings, where possible, are well-ventilated to allow them to 'breathe.' Large, roofed outdoor areas provide the opportunity for outdoor recreation, both within the high care facility and in central community spaces.

Environmental Sustainability and Energy Conservation

Rainwater is harvested and stored in large underground water tanks It is used for landscape irrigation and toilet flushing. The buildings are all designed with wide roof overhangs and awnings and screens on window openings to reduce heat gain. The apartments received an average 8-star BERS rating.

Design and Philosophy of Care

Holy Spirit's philosophy of care is about contributing positively to the lives of people who live there. The building delivers on this philosophy by providing a safe, secure, and high-quality environment where residents have the opportunity to participate in life in a supportive community to a level with which they feel comfortable.

Integration of Residents with the Broader Community

Stage 2 provides community facilities for both the RACF and Retirement Apartments. It provides a new front door for the site, while the shaded plaza will become the social hub for the site. Various community spaces are accessed from the plaza, including the chapel, function room, café, hairdresser, and gym.

In line with its status as the focal point for the site, the community center is designed to be colorful, appealing, and appropriate for its tropical setting. It is designed to draw the wider community into the site.

Project Capacity and Numbers of Units

Independent living apartments (units) 38 completed, 100 planned

Skilled nursing care (beds) 86

Kitchen (daily meals served) 400

Fitness/rehab/wellness (daily visits) 20

Breakdown of Independent Living Units

Two bedroom units 34

Typical size per unit 100m²

Two bedroom plus units 4

Typical size per unit 125m²

Breakdown of Skilled Nursing Care Units

One bed/single occupancy rooms 86

Typical size per unit 17m², with 5m² ensuite

Opposite A wide palette of materials and colour reflect the tropical context.

Left Wide overhangs provide shade and protection from rainfall.

Below Landscaping provides opportunities for a variety of intimate spaces.

Huruan Shimei Bay Residences

Shimei Bay, China

**China Resources Shimei Bay Tourism Development /
three**: living architecture

Project type Active Senior/
Independent Living Residence,
Assisted Living/Hostel Residence,
Community-Based Services,
Multi-Level Care/Continuing Care
Retirement Communities

Site size 56,625m²

Site location Suburban

Building footprint 11,533m²

Building area 46,490m²

Date completed August 2015

Owner's Statement

The development site is surrounded by Xiling Park to the north and east, by existing high-rise residential buildings to the west, and by the main resort road to the south. An organic layout of residences and buildings of differing scales and purposes must create well-designed and purposeful plazas, function courts, and common areas, to be enjoyed by elder residents, visitors, and the general public. Care was taken in segregating pedestrian, vehicular, and service circulation on the site.

Architect's Statement

Shimei Bay is a special place in a spectacular, natural environment surrounded by forested mountains and two natural rivers flowing into the vast and beautiful sea. The oxygen-rich forest and the life-sustaining rivers promote an atmosphere of health, wellness, and life. This natural and organic setting influences the master planning of the site where the buildings, pathways, and created spaces are highly organic and dynamic.

Just as life is a journey, a main pathway traverses throughout the site and is used as a metaphor for the twists and turns and changes that each individual experiences in life. The main pathway begins at the base of the mountain and meanders through the Commons or 'heart' of the community, emptying into the Retail Plaza and connecting the guest with the pedestrian path and roadway, which lead to other areas of Shimei Bay. The pedestrian circulation is thoughtfully planned to promote a wonderful sequence of spaces, where discovery and different experiences enhance the daily lives of the residents and create opportunities for many functions and events.

Finally, this project, like each person's life, will tell a story where life and journey intersect in this very special place. The story that this development should tell is one of a transformational living experience that can be shared and enjoyed from generation to generation.

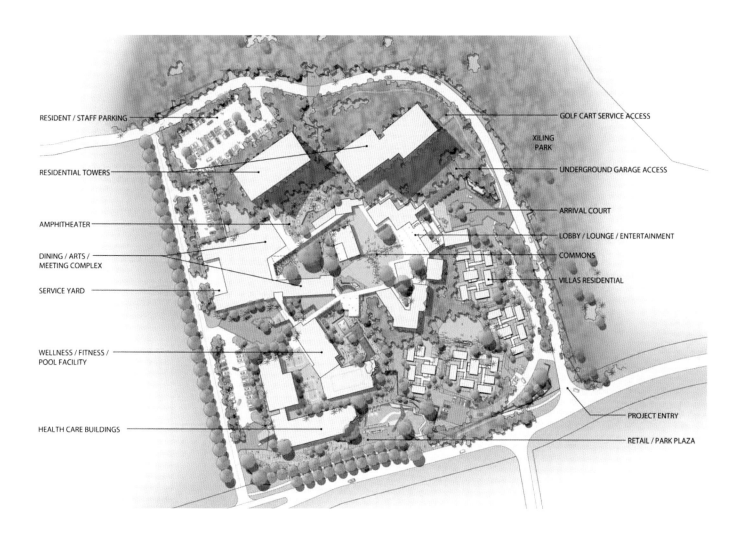

RESIDENT / STAFF PARKING

RESIDENTIAL TOWERS

AMPHITHEATER

DINING / ARTS /
MEETING COMPLEX

SERVICE YARD

WELLNESS / FITNESS /
POOL FACILITY

HEALTH CARE BUILDINGS

GOLF CART SERVICE ACCESS

XILING
PARK

UNDERGROUND GARAGE ACCESS

ARRIVAL COURT

LOBBY / LOUNGE / ENTERTAINMENT

COMMONS

VILLAS RESIDENTIAL

PROJECT ENTRY

RETAIL / PARK PLAZA

Above Overall site plan

Client Goals and Design Team Solutions

1 **Client Goal:** 'Create a special place.'

Design team solution: The concept for the development is derived from the words 'life, journey, and story.' Each of these words is important to the philosophy of the conceptual design so that each guest will experience the beauty and wonder associated with Shimei Bay. The pathway and circulation journey through the site is a metaphor for the changes that each individual experiences in life.

2 **Client Goal:** 'Integrate elder residents with public amenities.'

Design team solution: The design team has included and featured many interior and exterior spaces that integrate private and public usage. Functional areas include the Retail Plaza, Health Care Complex, and Wellness and Fitness—all of which are open to the public. In addition, the Sky Level Restaurant, also open to the public, sits high above the development site on top of one of the residential towers and provides memorable experiences for residents and guests alike.

3 **Client Goal:** 'Create an organic, hospitality-based collection of buildings and spaces.'

Design team solution: The seemingly casual arrangement of site components is carefully crafted to provide unique and distinguished courts and entertaining areas. On-grade service circulation is limited, while most of the service functions occur below grade and out of site, in true hospitality fashion. Vehicular circulation is limited to the perimeter of the site, providing a truly pedestrian atmosphere.

Left Aerial rendering

Environmental Sustainability & Energy Conservation

Extensive solar studies were performed to ensure that as many interior and exterior spaces as possible received maximum daylight, which in turn helped to minimize energy costs and consumption. Water runoff from mountains to the north is collected and stored on-site and used for landscape irrigation.

Design & Philosophy of Care

By using innovative design, the philosophy of senior care and services is expressive of the paradigm shift of senior living of the future. The design is hospitality-based, yet informed by senior living concepts. 'Living' means transformational experiences, and catering to guests' and residents' desires. Instead of creating an isolated environment, the architect has created a place with a greater purpose—attracting family members and interacting with society.

Similarly, the hospitality service mindset and operations are quite different from the health care service mindset and model. This becomes evident in the earliest stages of selection and training of caregivers and staff.

Integration of Residents with the Broader Community

A Retail Plaza, anchoring the south side of the site development, is one of the main design integrators of elder residents with the broader community. In addition, Wellness and Fitness includes a Health Care component available to the community, as well as indoor and outdoor pools, and activity areas for elders and children alike. Atop one of the Independent Living residential towers is the Sky Level Restaurant, which is open to the public and invites dramatic views to the mountains and to Shimei Bay to the south.

Project Capacity and Numbers of Units

Independent living apartments 300

Independent living cottages/villas (units) 4

Assisted living/hostel care (units) 20

Kitchen (daily meals served) 750

Elder outreach (clients) 75

Fitness/rehab/wellness (daily visits) 300

Pool(s) and related areas (daily visits) 300

Breakdown of Independent Living Units

Studio/bed-sit units 24
Typical size per unit 45m²

One bedroom units 96
Typical size per unit 80m²

Two bedroom units 180
Typical size per unit 100m²

Two bedroom plus units 4
Typical size per unit 200m²

Breakdown of Assisted Living/Hostel Care Units

Studio/bed-sit units 5
Typical size per unit 33m²

One bedroom units 15
Typical size per unit 60m²

Opposite Residential suite interior concept

Above Conceptual perspective of children's play pool

Lenbrook

Atlanta, Georgia, USA
Lenbrook Foundation, Inc. / THW Design

Project type Multi-Level Care/
Continuing Care Retirement
Communities
Site location Urban
Site size 2.65 hectares
Building footprint 16,260m²
Building area 60,240m²
Total building cost US$124 million
Building cost US$2,056/m²
Date completed October 2009
Photography courtesy of the
architect

Owner's Statement

Lenbrook was conceived by an Atlanta businessman, who in the early 1980s decided to build an upscale, full-service retirement community in the desirable Buckhead neighborhood. The new venture began, and the community opened to its first residents in July 1983. The original site sat on a 1.4-hectare plot and accommodated 225 residents. After 20 years, owners wanted to ensure continued success of the community by adding more convenience to residents by expanding services and amenities with state-of-the-art modifications. Lenbrook received the necessary permits and funding to proceed with 142 new residences, a Wellness Center and Spa and the renovation of existing community areas. The facility acquired an adjacent land parcel of one hectare, allowing the construction and planning phases to begin.

Right Aerial view
Opposite Arrival view

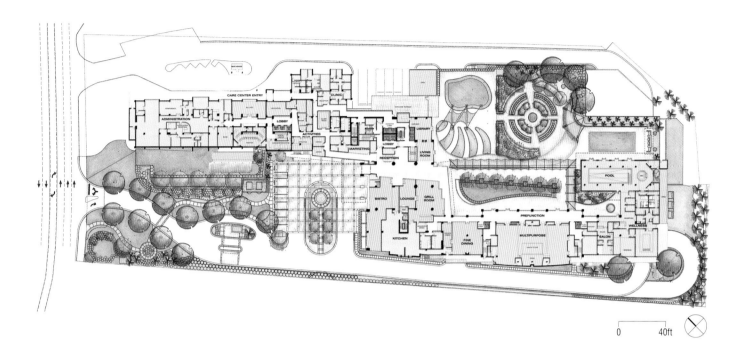

0   40ft

Architect's Statement

The client knew that to remain viable, they needed to engage in a renovation and expansion program to meet the significant and growing demand for in-town living opportunities. A philosophy and value system that the design team understood was the imperative need to create multiple "social hubs," because happy and engaged residents are also healthier ones. Lenbrook's US$124 million expansion (two phases) consists of a magnificent 25-story building with sweeping views of downtown. This project hosts 142 Independent Living homes, 16 Assisted Living, and 60 in Skilled Care, 20 of which are memory-focused.

Among the amenities on the campus are three-level townhouse plans, as well as an elegant garden court building overlooking a 3,530m² tranquil landscaped plaza. This plaza serves as the social hub for multi-generational

social connectivity. Three upscale dining venues were added, a 465m² multi-purpose room, and a state-of-the-art video theater. Additionally, a 995m² fully equipped Wellness Center and Spa, and glass-enclosed natatorium complete with heated pool are available for resident indulgence.

This urban mixed-use development not only serves the needs of seniors seeking fashionable in-town community living, but also provides a platform for assorted social confluence opportunities in the heart of Atlanta's prestigious Buckhead community. Lenbrook is Atlanta's only nationally accredited Continuing Care Retirement Community (CCRC). Lenbrook offers the city-dwelling 50+ population various distinguished upscale living choices, complete with lifestyle packages geared to entice the most discerning of consumers. The design team comprised Mark Tilden and Song Cheng.

Client Goals and Design Team Solutions

1 Client goal: Introduce new state-of-the-art residences and amenities that will reposition Lenbrook and create long-term viability.

Design team solution: Comprising just some of the newly added components are a 465m² multi-purpose room, a billiards room, a two-tiered video theater, a postal center, a convenience store, full service bank, resident business center, fully equipped 995m² Wellness Center, day spa, and glass enclosed natatorium with heated swimming pool. Three new dining venues were also added to offer even more resident choice options. Lenbrook wanted residents who chose to live there to feel that within their community home, they are offered service packages similar to that of a resort. In addition to the many amenities the community offers, concierge service is abundant throughout.

2 Client goal: Create multiple social hubs that support a philosophy and value system that engages active residents, making them happier and healthier.

Design team solution: In addition to the various internal common space renovations and additions, the design fashioned "outdoor rooms" created specifically for resident wellness. Intergenerational connectivity opportunities are abundant in the socially engaging Wellness Plaza. This plaza is the true epicenter of community activity. A plethora of activities can be held here, such as crisp fall evening marshmallow roasts on the fire pit, wine and hors d'oeuvres by the outdoor kitchen, peaceful strolls in the plaza garden, and outdoor sporting events.

3 Client goal: Create a center of innovation and excellence in senior living that reflects a new urban environment.

Design team solution: Contemporary design elements are thoughtfully blended with existing traditional structures, and the design team needed to create a smooth and cohesive mix between the varying styles. In addition to the glass-enclosed natatorium, the residential tower has a sleek, modern flair with glass and concrete structuring; other elements have a more traditional appeal. Common space interiors present a comfortable and inviting setting with elegant furnishings, reflecting timeless sensibility. The new town-homes will emulate "New England" style, and will be adjacent to the community's two high-rise towers, creating an interesting and welcoming community feel.

Major Design Objectives and/or Project Challenges and the Related Responses

1 Meeting tricky and restrictive zoning height and set-back limitations that would satisfy the building integration requirement: From the rear of the existing building tower to the beginning of the new expansion tower, a 35-metre gap had to be created to link the differing floor heights of the two buildings. A removal of the first four bays of the existing parking structure was thus required. The remaining parking structure was then extended to the west, which doubled the size, and which now accommodates more parking. Atop the western side of the parking structure is a three-story Garden Court wing, tailored to fit within the allocated narrow area. Now the parking is improved, and the buildings are properly and seamlessly connected.

2 Creating a high-rise structure without impairing views: The client wanted to create a new high-rise structure that would not impair the views that the existing homeowners were already enjoying in the existing tower. The new tower was oriented east and west, slightly behind the old tower, to preserve existing resident views with the smallest dimension facing the adjacent neighborhood to mitigate their concerns about the view being impaired. It was important to Lenbrook that the existing residents could enjoy views of the city skyline and Stone Mountain unhindered by the new construction.

3 Adapting to changing resident needs: There are a total of 360 independent living apartments that are adaptable to changing resident needs spread between the two buildings and the Garden Courts. An example of this would be the roll-in showers, to accommodate changing mobility levels. Like most communities, this one is challenged by issues associated with aging in place. Trauma is endured by the residents when they are moved along a continuum, in a system that supports the community's needs over the residents'. While providing adequate care to the residents is of pivotal importance, so is the security and inner wellbeing of the individuals. The owner challenged the designer to create living accommodations that would allow residents to have a comfortable amount of space and amenities more consistent with independent living quarters, for all residents. Many Assisted Living homes have been designed for couples to remain together, despite differing healthcare needs.

Opposite top Penthouse floor plan
Opposite middle Typical floor plan
Opposite bottom Typical skilled care floor plan

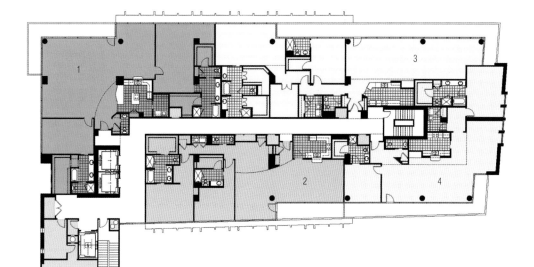

1 Tuxedo
2 Chatham
3 Habersham
4 Ansley

1 Windsor
2 Ivy
3 Wieuca
4 Cherokee
5 Andrews
6 Wesley
7 Stratford

1 Residences
2 Staff commons
3 Living
4 Dining
5 Activities
6 Lounge
7 Resident commons

Unique Context

Lenbrook is Atlanta's only nationally accredited CCRC. Lenbrook provides upscale accommodations and lifestyle amenities for the 50+ residents within an urban mixed-use development in the heart of Atlanta. Contemporary architectural design in a sleek concrete and glass residential tower offers expansive and dynamic views of the city skyline. The modern design elements add a fresh twist and urban appeal to senior housing within the city. The large scale landscaping materials installed gives this community an immediate sense of maturity and sophistication. Landscape and hardscape are carefully blended to enhance the entrance to the site as well as to the centralized social Wellness Plaza, which provides outdoor activity areas for the residents, staff, and their families. Nestled in the heart of Atlanta's affluent Buckhead community, residents here are but a stone's throw away from trendy dining hot spots and Atlanta's most premiere shopping. Finally, this community was designed with social confluence opportunities in mind for the residents.

Environmental Sustainability & Energy Conservation

The renovation and expansion of Lenbrook was designed with sustainability in mind. The owner chose to go with high-performance glazing for this project, which has significant benefits. Not only does it achieve lower energy bills, but it cuts out 92 per cent of the sun's ultraviolet rays, while eliminating the blazing heat of the Atlanta summer sun. In addition, this project has extensive natural landscaping, green roofs, and on-site storm water collection. Sustainability, resident comfort, and protecting the environment are core principles for both the owner and THW Design.

Integration of Residents with the Broader Community

Located in the Buckhead community of metropolitan Atlanta, a topography known for affluence and fast paced city life, the owner wanted to harness all the attributes of high-rise living in an exciting city, while also offering residents a private and comforting sanctuary to call home. Centrally located, Lenbrook's residents will have immediate access to public transportation, although the city's trendiest hot spots are a stone's throw away. From quaint cafes to designer shopping, engaging accoutrements are at their disposal. While at Lenbrook, residents are afforded the in-town indulgences that they expect, but they are also granted a hidden gem in the city, with tranquil and unexpected lush landscape and expansive green space.

Staffing

Total number of staff at this project/facility 240

Number of management staff 15

Number of care staff (registered nursing and direct care staff) 86

Direct care hours per day per client 4.4

Number of other staff (e.g. maintenance, housekeeping, food services) 108

Project Capacity and Numbers of Units

Independent living apartments 142 new, 360 in total

Assisted living/hostel care 16

Skilled nursing care (beds) 40

Kitchen (daily meals served) 874

Fitness/rehab/wellness (daily visits) 80

Pool(s) and related areas (daily visits) 18

Breakdown of Independent Living Units

One bedroom units 75
Typical size per unit 79m²

Two bedroom units 208
Typical size per unit 120m²

Two bedroom plus units 77
Typical size per unit 156m²

Breakdown of Assisted Living/Hostel Care Units

One bedroom units 16
Typical size per unit 58m²

Breakdown of Dementia Special Care Units

Studio/bed-sit units 20
Typical size per unit 27m²

Breakdown of Skilled Nursing Care Units

One bed/single occupancy rooms 40

Typical size per unit 27m²

Resident/Client Age

Current average age 85.3 years old

Age upon entry 81.2 years old

Resident/Client Fees and Funding

Entry fee Yes

Client monthly funding Private (out-of-pocket) pay

Lenbrook is the premier not-for-profit CCRC located in Atlanta, Georgia. Lenbrook was the first community in Georgia to receive CARF-CCAC accreditation and is still the only one accredited in the city of Atlanta.

Lenbrook comprises 360 apartments for independent living residents; 16 Personal Care Suites and a 60-bed skilled nursing center. All levels are private pay; however, due to the very recent Medicare approval of the SNF, Lenbrook will begin to receive Medicare reimbursement for appropriate admissions.

The current residents of Lenbrook range in age from 66 to 99 (65 is the minimum age for admission). Females outnumber males by approximately two to one.

Lenbrook promotes resident independence, good health, and personal fulfillment and supports the access to appropriate services to allow our residents to live full and engaged lives. A variety of classes, speakers, outings, and entertainment are available for a wide spectrum of diverse offerings. These are designed to promote social, spiritual, and physical whole-personal wellness to residents across the continuum of care. Dining choices promote variety and range from casual quick comfort foods to upscale cuisine comparable to fine restaurants in the city.

Resident input is encouraged and the resident association leadership and committees make a viable contribution to many aspects of life at Lenbrook.

Opposite Formal dining

Left Natatorium

Lifestyle Manor Bondi

Bondi, New South Wales, Australia

Australian Unity / Campbell Luscombe Architects

Project type Active Senior/
Independent Living Residence
Site Location Urban
Site size 2,880m²
Building footprint 1,315m² (Level 1)
Building area 5,654m²
Building cost AUS$3,020/m²
Date completed September 2008
Photography Brett Boardman
Photography

Owner's Statement

Located in the heart of Sydney's prestigious eastern suburbs and only moments from vibrant Bondi, Lifestyle Manor was to be a prestige retirement apartment development in a truly magnificent location. The creation of beautiful shared spaces to enjoy, and a range of services and facilities add a touch of luxury to retirement. The owners envisaged a retirement community that would enable their residents to experience the very best of city living, in a secure vibrant environment.

An abundance of surrounding boutique retailers, cafés, bookshops, galleries, and restaurants would extend the lifestyle quality of the envisaged extensive in-house facilities. Lifestyle Manor offers a range of domestic and dining services, giving residents more free time to spend doing the things they enjoy the most.

Should the residents' needs change over time, quality care and professional support are available at every stage from Australian Unity, a name with a longstanding tradition of providing for the needs of older Australians.

Right Rear apartments looking over Bondi

Opposite Apartment balconies facing north

98

Above Ground floor plan
Opposite Internal central atrium

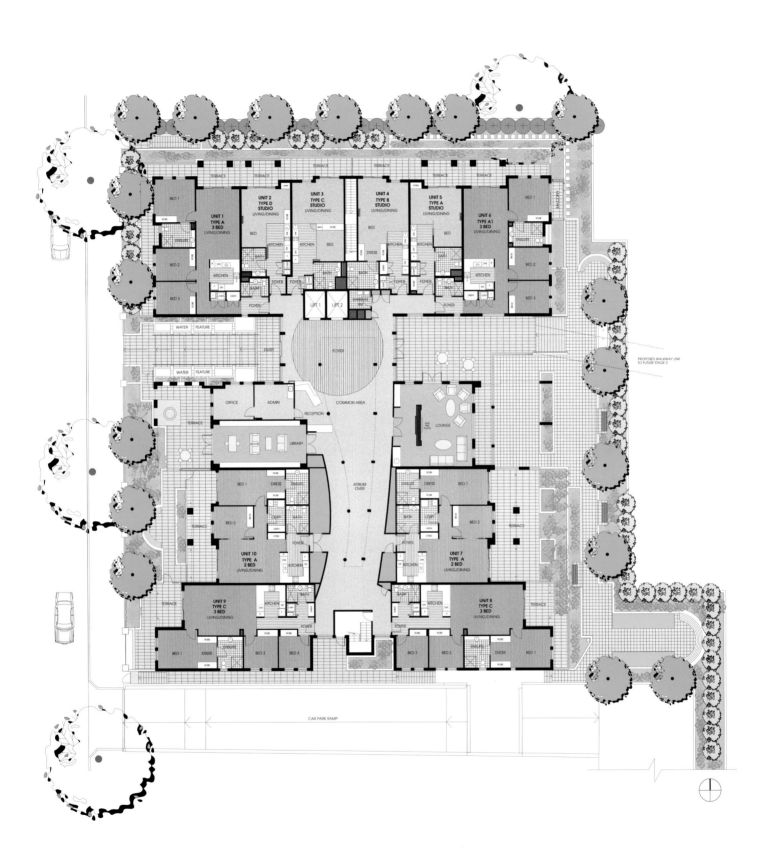

Architect's Statement

Lifestyle Manor Bondi is a unique advance in Australian retirement living. Taking advantage of the lively, urban context of Sydney's eastern suburbs, the development strategy transformed what could have simply been 'a block of flats' that happened to be occupied by elderly people into a vital and engaging seniors community.

The core of the development of 42 luxury, one, two and three bedroom apartments is the glass-roofed central atrium passing through five of the building's seven levels, giving true life to the concept of the 'vertical village.'

By internally revealing resident activity over five levels, the sense of physical, social, and visual communication reinforces communality (the sense of 'belonging') and creates a positive and activating atmosphere.

The development's luxury facilities incorporate a rooftop dining room with terrace for entertaining, a lower level cinema, gym, hair salon and treatment room, function center, arts and crafts workshop, medical consulting suite, heated swimming pool, and on the main lobby level a library, and an intimate lounge space.

The style of the building was developed to respond to the aesthetic aspirations and memories of senior residents by utilizing a dignified contemporary interpretation of Sydney's 'grand' apartment buildings of the 1920s.

Below 'Hotel-style' entry/reception
Right Level 2 floor plan
Opposite left Level 5 floor plan
Opposite right Glazed roof to central atrium

Client Goals and Design Team Solutions

1   **Client goal:** To create a community.

Design team solution: The five-level central atrium is the internal heart of the building, and is the primary architectural element used to achieve that sense of physical, social, and visual communication that is necessary in a seniors community.

2   **Client goal:** Maximize the potential of the site location and create a boutique, prestige retirement development.

Design team solution: The site, located within a dense existing urban context, required the new building to be a 'good neighbor' first and foremost. While slightly taller than some of its surrounding context, by utilizing the fall of site, and creating underground parking, it managed to present a complimentary character to the street, achieving a natural yet prestigious contextual fit.

3   **Client goal:** Maximize the ESD potential of the development.

Design team solution: The five-level (with two additional basement parking levels) building, is unique in the senior housing sector and reflects an intelligent response to environmental and sustainability issues. The development's ESD strategy maximizes the number of corner apartments with increased access to natural daylighting and cross-ventilation and incorporates rainwater harvesting, a graywater recycling system, solar hot water, and thermal stack ventilation.

Major Design Objectives and/or Project Challenges and the Related Responses

1 To ensure a vibrant seniors community: The core objective was to ensure a vibrant community, not merely a collection of dwellings inhabited by elderly people. The five-level central atrium is the internal heart of the building,

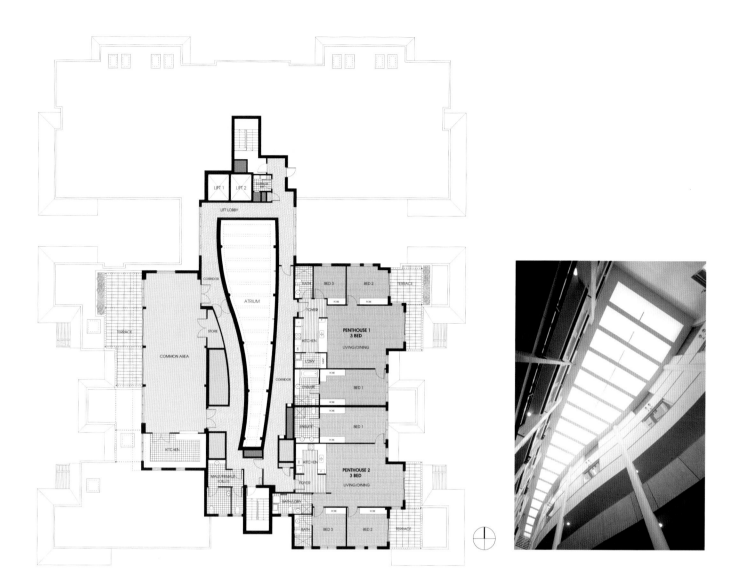

and is the primary architectural element used to achieve that sense of physical, social, and visual communication that is necessary within a seniors community.

By internally revealing resident activity over five levels, the sense of physical, social and visual communication reinforces communality, (the sense of 'belonging') and creates a positive and activating atmosphere, dispelling isolation. The atrium is like a vertical 'village square' supporting the ability to meet, mingle, and share.

2 Maximizing the ecologically sustainable development (ESD) potential of the development: While the intention was to be as environmentally responsible as possible, it was not the intention to be a visible 'showcase' of sustainability. The sustainable initiatives would always be subtly evident, never visually dominating the sense of quiet comfort and character. As already noted above, the development's ESD strategy maximizes the number of corner apartments with increased access to natural day-lighting and cross-ventilation and incorporates rainwater harvesting, a graywater recycling system, solar hot water, and thermal stack ventilation.

3 Architectural character: The project was to attract as much by the quality of its dwellings and the variety of its facilities, as by the character of the building itself. The style of the building was developed to respond to the aesthetic aspirations and cultural memories of senior residents, particularly those resident in or familiar with the surrounding suburban context, by utilizing a dignified contemporary interpretation of many of the 'grand' apartment buildings of the 1920s, many found in the nearby city center and areas adjacent to it. It was to be a truly urban seniors community.

Unique Context

The urban retirement/seniors community is not common within the Sydney context. Most independent living developments for seniors generally find themselves on the outer fringe of the metropolis or occasionally in some of the established low-density middle suburbs. Obviously this is driven as much by land cost as it is by population proximity.

Bondi is located in the relatively narrow residential area (The Eastern Suburbs) between the city center and the Pacific Ocean. (The famous Bondi Beach is less than 1.5 kilometers from the site). The development pattern in this area is a mix of small, tight single-lot dwellings often closely adjacent to medium and high-rise apartments. By the nature of land value in this area, and the rarity of a moderately large site (the site was formerly a redundant private school), the development market for seniors dwellings would always fall within the higher end of the socio-economic spectrum.

While in close proximity to some of Sydney's most affluent residential areas, Bondi has maintained to certain extent a 'raffish beach culture' environment. However, the inevitable recognition over the last 30 years of Bondi's proximity to the retail, cultural, and lifestyle centers of Sydney has ensured its rise in real estate desirability.

Other project information

The initial development team saw the potential for a prestigious seniors community in an area where little had previously been provided. The project was subsequently bought out by one of Australia's largest health providers, extending their portfolio of seniors developments. This ownership permitted the extension of services available to the current and future residents. The project was selected as a finalist in the NSW section of the Urban Development Institute of Australia (NSW) 'Urban Development Awards – Retirement Living.'

Environmental Sustainability & Energy Conservation

As noted above, the building reflects an intelligent response to environmental and sustainability issues. The development's ESD strategy maximizes the number of corner apartments with increased access to natural day-lighting and cross-ventilation by maximizing the number of aspects these apartments address. Passive sustainability—i.e. good orientation, carefully designed sun access and shielding—limit the dependence on mechanical environmental support.

Gardens and landscaping are watered from rainwater harvesting stored in basement tanks and reticulated throughout the site. This is supplemented by a graywater recycling system, rooftop mounted solar assisted hot water and the projects central apartments having access to thermal stack ventilation, providing cross-ventilation even to the centrally located single aspect units.

Advanced Technology

As well as necessary emergency notification access facilities, the project provides residents with all the modern communication and lifestyle technology expected in high-end residential developments.

Design & Philosophy of Care

While the project is an independent living development, the building accommodates facilities that provide dining and additional domestic services at request by the residents. The philosophy of care also extends to the extensive wellness center and indoor heated swimming pool that forms the core of the resident facilities.

Integration of Residents with the Broader Community

The project, by its location and target market, was always intended to attract its residents from the local surrounding area. Subsequently, an easy integration of residents with the broader community was achievable, most living within proximity of their existing cultural, retail, and lifestyle centers.

While being a private community, the public spaces are often opened to the public for community functions, most notably the ground level areas of the large atrium space are used as an art gallery, hanging works by local artists and hosting community charitable events.

Opposite Apartment kitchen
Top left Intimate resident lounge off the central atrium
Top right Apartment ensuite bathroom

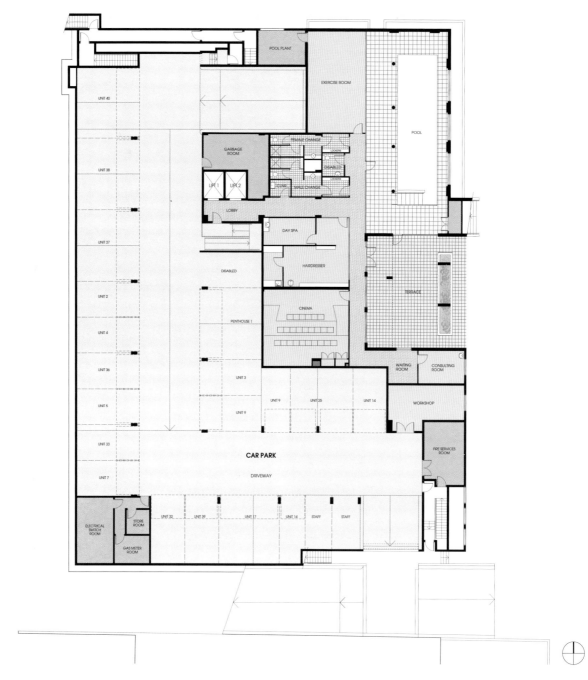

Labels in floor plan:

UNIT 40

POOL PLANT

EXERCISE ROOM

POOL

UNIT 38

FEMALE CHANGE

GARBAGE ROOM

LOCKERS

LIFT 1 LIFT 2

DISABLED

CLNR

MALE CHANGE

LOCKERS

UNIT 37

LOBBY

DAY SPA

UNIT 2

DISABLED

HAIRDRESSER

TERRACE

UNIT 4

PENTHOUSE 1

CINEMA

UNIT 36

UNIT 3

UNIT 5

UNIT 9

UNIT 9

UNIT 25

UNIT 14

WAITING ROOM

CONSULTING ROOM

WORKSHOP

UNIT 33

CAR PARK

FIRE SERVICES ROOM

UNIT 7

DRIVEWAY

ELECTRICAL SWITCH ROOM

STORE ROOM

UNIT 32

UNIT 39

UNIT 17

UNIT 14

STAFF

STAFF

GAS METER ROOM

Staffing

Total number of staff at this project/facility 4

Number of management staff 2

Number of other staff (e.g. maintenance, housekeeping, food services) 5

Project Capacity and Numbers of Units

Independent living apartments 42

Kitchen (daily meals served) Available as required

Fitness/rehab/wellness (daily visits) The facilities include a swimming pool, Fitness Centre, and consulting facilities

Pool(s) and related areas (daily visits) Indoor heated swimming pool within the facilities area of the development

Breakdown of Independent Living Units

Studio/bed-sit units 4
Typical size per unit 48m^2

One bedroom units 1
Typical size per unit 60m^2

Two bedroom units 24
Typical size per unit 95m^2

Two bedroom plus units 13
Typical size per unit 115m^2

Resident/Client Age

Current average age approximately 80 years old
Age upon entry approximately 76 years old

Resident/Client Fees and Funding

Entry fee or unit purchase Yes

Client monthly funding Private (out-of-pocket) pay

Public/Government funded No

Public/Government subsidies (means tested based on assets and/or income) No

The population of Lifestyle Manor Bondi is predominantly retired couples. Most residents have been local private business owners. All units are purchased, with prices in the upper percentile of the Sydney real estate market.

Opposite top Basement level 1 floor plan

Opposite bottom Indoor heated pool

Left Beauty & hairdresser

Below Fitness center exercise room

Mountain View Cohousing

Mountain View, California, USA
445 Calderon LLC / McCamant & Durrett Architects

Project type Active Senior/
Independent Living Residence,
Community-Based Services,
Senior Cohousing

Site location Urban, suburban

Site size 0.49 hectares

Building footprint 1,345m²

Building area 3,550m²

Total building cost US$6.5 million

Building cost US$1,830/m²

Date completed Scheduled for 2014

Photography Charles Durrett

Owner's Statement

Mountain View is a senior cohousing community, allowing seniors to age-in-place and preventing institutionalized care. Cohousing communities are unique in their extensive use of common facilities and—more importantly—in that they are organized, planned, and managed by the residents themselves. Yet cohousing is distinctive in that each family or household has a separate dwelling and chooses how much he or she wants to participate in community activities.

Inspired by the book *Senior Cohousing: A Community Approach to Independent Living,* Mountain View Cohousing started with a group of eight families who designed their homes, provided financial backing for construction, and will soon live in their personalized home. The group's goals consisted of creating a viable long-term place to live within the community, enjoying the activities and benefits of downtown Mountain View, and creating a 'place of real values' with quality design, inherent sensitivity to the environment, and a sense of community not found in many other places.

It was essential for the physical design of the cohousing to create a sense of neighborhood, nodes for casual encounters, common facilities, a center, connective paths, inviting and useable open areas, the ability to be independent and have privacy, built-in quality of materials, green design, and aesthetic sensitivity.

Right Physical model showing Northwest façade

Opposite top Front street elevation of cohousing community

Opposite bottom Rendering of community entrance showing existing building and proposed new building

Architect's Statement

This group is building a neighborhood for seniors in the larger neighborhood of downtown Mountain View. The site is approximately 0.5 hectares, but deep and narrow—120 meters by 40 meters—giving less design flexibility than might be desired. Physically, the cohousing community is built around a core "common room," where homeowners socialize, sharing food, activities, and experiences. The setting has extensive landscaped grounds that provide recreation, gardening, and places for reflection.

The design includes 19 private condominiums, a resident caregiver, housed in their own small caregivers below-market rent (BMR) unit, to support its members, and two rooms for visiting guests.

An old single-family farmhouse, built in 1890, remains on the site that provides guest rooms, a caregiver suite, and a meeting room. The farmhouse was moved from the middle of the site to the southwest corner. As part of the workshop process, the group settled on a more traditional American Shingle Style, which is both warm and accessible. The architecture is formal in that it was originally a "crafty" type of Victorian architecture, but it allows for informality and even serendipity at the same time.

Opposite top North elevation; South elevation

Left Common balcony where residents can gather with their neighbors

Above Common balcony can also be used for private gatherings

Client Goals and Design Team Solutions

1 Client Goal: Creating a senior cohousing community.

Design team solution: With less than 10 senior cohousing communities in the United States, getting one approved can be a challenge. With the knowledge and experience of creating cohousing for 30 years, Mountain View Cohousing will be added to the list. There is a large pent-up demand for more senior cohousing.

2 Client Goal: Creating a "place of real values."

Design team solution: Each resident will have their own home and will have access to common facilities, including a kitchen, exercise room, meeting room, lounge, workshop, and more. Not only will residents have private space, but will also have public space to share with their friends.

3 Client Goal: Creating an active community.

Design team solution: The site includes extensive recreation space with gardens and walking paths. Residents get to interact with others, planning shopping excursions, events, and DIY projects. Located only a few blocks from downtown, the residents can walk to town and experience the lively neighborhood of Mountain View, California.

Major Design Objectives and/or Project Challenges and the Related Responses

1 Designing the community around a common core: The common house is always the center/core of the community, and it was no exception for Mountain View. This is where everyone gets together for common meals, games, and events. It is the hub of the site.

2 Designing a sustainable community: The design is energy efficient, using low toxic materials, maximizing daylight and ventilation, and utilizing passive heating and cooling strategies. All of these contribute to a low-maintenance design.

3 Designing a place for the community to flourish: By creating a welcoming community where interaction is key, the residents will enjoy a higher quality of life. Every private house is designed with the kitchen sink facing out towards the common walkways. This encourages neighborly interaction, where residents can invite friends over for a cup of coffee.

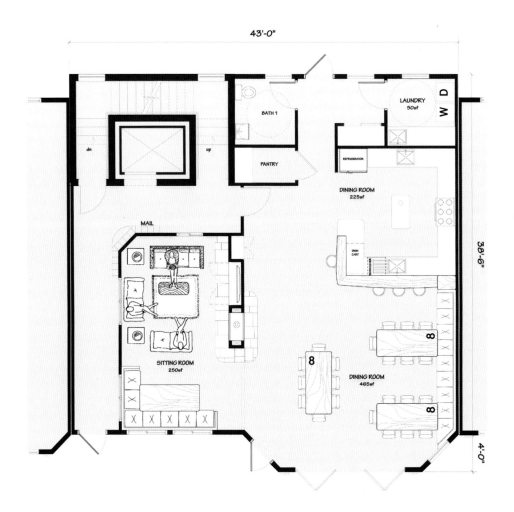

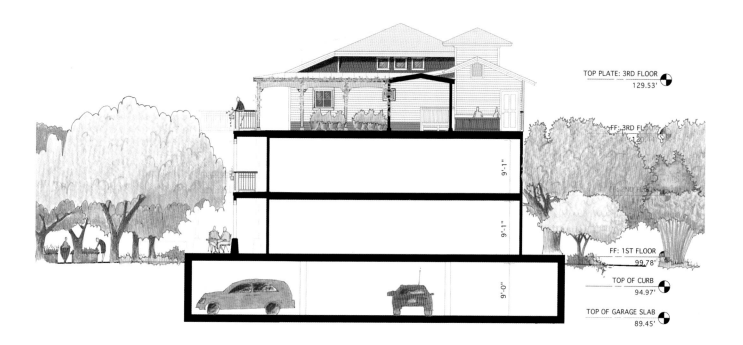

TOP PLATE: 3RD FLOOR
129.53'

FF: 3RD FLOOR

9'-1"

9'-1"

FF: 1ST FLOOR
99.78'

TOP OF CURB
94.97'

9'-0"

TOP OF GARAGE SLAB
89.45'

Opposite Common house floor plan
Above East section
Below Private house floor plan

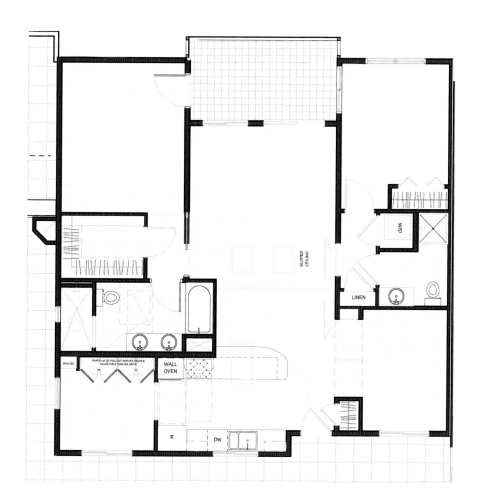

Unique Context

Mountain View Cohousing is a state-of-the-art neighborhood that offers its residents a sense of community, security, and a healthy lifestyle that enables them to successfully age in place. Compared to the alternative—living in single-family houses where they raised their family, but are not fit for a successful aging scenario, nor a sustainable future—seniors at Mountain View have figured it out.

Many seniors today do not have extended families nearby or stay-at-home children to take care of them, and there are few high-functioning small towns left. As a result, too many seniors are left with no other alternative than assisted living. A recent national study contends that 40 per cent of the seniors in assisted care today are prematurely institutionalized. Mountain View places a high-functional, sustainable, and affordable community that offers support, companionship, and fun within reach of those seniors who want to enjoy a vibrant small town community life.

Instead of sitting for hours a day watching television, the seniors at cohousing communities enjoy sitting on one of their front porches discussing the issues of the day or playing a board game with their neighbors over a cup of coffee or tea.

Environmental Sustainability & Energy Conservation

Cohousing communities occupy less than 30 per cent as much land as the average new subdivision. Mountain View Cohousing's site is small, yet long (0.49 hectares), running west to east. Although a challenging site, the buildings were oriented so the longest elevations faced north and south, maximizing daylight and cross ventilation. The footprint is small, allowing for ample outdoor space for recreation and land preservation. The cohousers can easily walk to downtown, nearby shops and restaurants, and public transportation stops. On average, the community drives about 60 per cent less than most Americans.

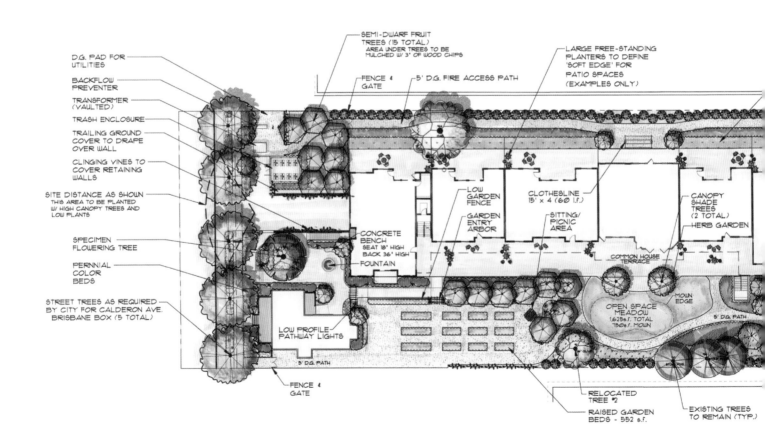

Above Landscape site plan by Jo McProud of McProud & Associates

Advanced Technology

The design for the community began from the very beginning. Advanced framing cuts down on material costs, allows for fewer breaks in the insulation, and increases the R-value of the wall. A radiant barrier on the roof to reflect the sun's rays away from the building will reduce heat gain. Solar panels will also be installed on the roof, collecting energy for each resident's home.

Design & Philosophy of Care

Today, almost 25 per cent of the American population lives alone, and this percentage is increasing as the number of Americans over the age of 60 increases. As with all cohousing communities, nobody is ever alone or lonely. You have a neighbor nearby all the time. These neighbors will not only help you out when needed, but will also check on you if you miss dinner one evening. The community consists of friends—people residents can trust and count on to cook dinner or play cards with.

Integration of Residents with the Broader Community

The site arrangement at Mountain View is most importantly conducive to embracing community. Its 'one-building' solution contributes to create positive outdoor spaces. The arrangement of the buildings provides a sense of entry that blends into the existing neighborhood, which is, at the same time, welcoming, yet private. The favorable location of Mountain View Cohousing, just within a few blocks from downtown Mountain View and its many amenities, fosters social connectivity and walkable accessibility. The open, not gated, design features edible gardens to one side of the site in an accessible space that allows for a social exchange between residents and neighbors. This combination allows for a positive social space that blends into the surrounding neighborhood and connects to the larger community.

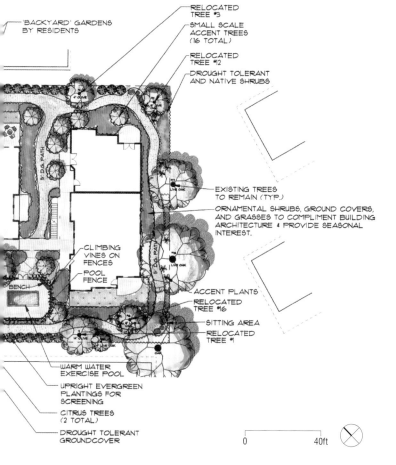

Project Capacity and Numbers of Units
Independent living apartments 19

Breakdown of Independent Living Units
Two bedroom plus units 19
Typical size per unit 166m²

Resident/Client Age
Average age upon entry between 55 and 80

Resident/Client Fees and Funding
Entry fee or unit purchase Yes
Client Monthly Funding Private (out-of-pocket) pay

Nambucca Heads
UnitingCare Ageing

Nambucca Heads, New South Wales, Australia
**UnitingCare Ageing NSW.ACT (North Coast Region) /
Campbell Luscombe Architects**

Owner's Statement

Project type Special Care Residence
(for those with dementia), Skilled
Nursing Care Residence

Site Location Small Town

Site Size 3,853m²

Building footprint 1,921m²

Building area 5,463m²

Total building cost N/A

Building cost AUS$3,300/m²

Date completed January 2012

Photography Jeremy Rogers
Photography

The project was one of two aged care facilities commissioned concurrently, approximately 90 kilometers apart on the mid-north coast of New South Wales, Australia. Crucial to the design is UnitingCare Ageing's commitment to creating a home-like environment that is deinstitutionalized and fosters a person-centered care approach. It is envisaged that this concept will look like a collection of individual communities within a residential care facility, with small, warm community clusters that have all the features of a home-like environment. Service facilities such as serveries, kitchens, and pan rooms should be strategically positioned to avoid creating an institutional environment but aim at servicing the maximum numbers of residents.

As within a town concept, the community areas such as chapel, shop, hairdressers, and libraries should be in a central hub to create a feeling of adventure and outing for residents and located on the level with the maximum number of residents for ease of access. The residential facility design should allow residents to feel they are at home and have the ability to access all elements of service, with the independence and warmth which they currently enjoy in their everyday lives.

The architectural design of the building should maximize harmony with the surrounding natural environment and offer a stylish spacious lifestyle. It was anticipated that the view from the rooftop recreation terraces of 'Pacifica' to the scenic surrounding hills would offer residents a relaxing, secure outdoor entertaining area.

Right Central wing to street

Opposite Covered entry with residential wings beyond

Architect's Statement

UnitingCare Ageing's strategy to satisfy the need for aged care services on the mid-north coast of NSW, was rather than provide one large facility, the client decided to develop two independent sites concurrently, one at Port Macquarie, New South Wales, 300 kilometers north of Sydney, and a second, 90 kilometers further up the coast at Nambucca Heads. The design needed to respond carefully to UnitingCare Ageing's recently implemented Service and Care models. However, the particulars of the individual sites necessitated individual responses to each facility.

The design sought to embody the concept of 'normalcy,' to reflect a home setting rather than an institutional facility. Despite being quite a large building within its context, the layout discarded the 'healthcare' environment to provide a calm home-like ambiance. The building was structured into separate resident wings, largely located on different levels, creating individual care units as 'houses.' Each house with its own legible 'front door' and entry, and its own kitchen is reinforced by a strong linear hierarchy of privacy, from front door to bedroom.

The Nambucca Heads site was (for an aged care facility) steeply falling but relatively close to the town center. The resolution required a building stepped and terraced over five levels to best utilize the site and to take advantage of the resulting roof terraces. Both facilities became operational in 2012.

Above Lounge/sitting room of an individual house
Opposite top 'Estuary Terrace Café' at ground level
Opposite bottom Lower ground floor

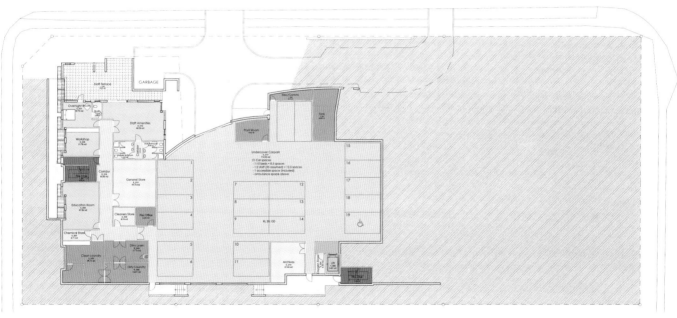

Client Goals and Design Team Solutions

1 Client goal: To develop the 'household' model of care.

Design team solution: The architectural resolution entailed the division of the 86 residential bedrooms into either separate wings or to be on different levels, each housing between 16 to 20 beds. Each 'house' wing (actually a U-shaped configuration to minimize corridor length) contained its own legible front door and private lobby space, a sitting and dining area for the 'house,' a fully equipped domestic kitchen and a collection of additional small sitting/lounge areas, which further breaks down the feeling of an institution.

The 'house' domestic kitchen, while functional in itself, was used as a servery for meals brought to the 'house' from the central in-house commercial kitchen. The necessary service areas associated with nursing care, utility rooms, nurses stations, additional toilets, among other facilities, are all discreetly located and are imperceptible to the ambiance of the domestic environment.

2 Client goal: The 'town concept' of residences and services.

Design team solution: Outside the residential 'houses,' the facility provides two distinct categories of support space. Firstly, the resident community spaces; therapy and consulting rooms, a hairdressing salon, a library, a chapel, and a café are generally concentrated and located adjacent to or off the main building entry to encourage the residents to leave their 'house' and create a feeling of an outing.

Secondly, the necessary back-of-house components, that include staff and education facilities, the commercial-sized kitchen and laundry, that serve the entire facility have been located at the rear and are serviced from the basement and do not form part of the public and resident experience of the building.

Major Design Objectives and/or Project Challenges and the Related Responses

1 The home-like environment: To reinforce the perception of home, each resident should feel their space defined through their domestic surrounds. The major challenge to the residential aged care facility is that the necessarily large infrastructure needed to service the medical and residential needs of a great number of frail elderly people in an economically viable manner, can so easily become institutional and hospital-like. The solution largely disguises that infrastructure in support of the small scale and individual. As outlined above, as well as the creation of smaller residential clusters and the small

intimate spaces it contains. Meals prepared in the central kitchen are brought from this kitchen to each house, where it is 'served' from the small domestic kitchen within each individual 'house' cluster.

2 Architectural character: Nambucca Heads is a small, relaxed coastal town. By the nature of the size of this facility, it would inevitably be a large building within the surrounding small town seaside context and the relatively steep site ensured a stepped building over five levels. Subsequently the mass of the building is fragmented and disguised as it steps down the fall of the land. The upper levels utilize roof terraces and the majority of rooms embrace two sun-filled courtyards, which promoted an architecture that embraces light and openness.

3 To embrace the local community: The proximity of the 'Pacifica' site to the local town center offered opportunities to make the facility more open to the local community. Within the limits of ensuring a secure environment for the residents of Pacifica, a ground-level welcoming café and garden terrace were incorporated into the design from an early stage. Given the steepness of the site and its relative smallness, most outdoor recreational space was created from the security of roof terraces, which ensures a degree of openness not often found in aged care facilities.

Unique Context

The 'Pacifica' client, a 'not-for-profit' organization, is a division of a major church, and is one of Australia's largest providers of aged care services. The client prides itself on its care models and the research it undertakes on international trends in aged services, and is often at the forefront of aged care provision in Australia.

Nambucca Heads is a small relaxed coastal town on the mid-north coast of New South Wales, approximately 400 kilometers north of Sydney. The site was originally a small retirement community of a few houses adjacent to the local church. The site is bounded by three public roads and a private driveway at the rear, with the long axis of the site facing north. The surrounding context is a mixture of suburban on the edge of the town center, with another seniors retirement village behind. The site was very tight for the accommodation required and subsequently the multi-level solution with the utilization of roof terraces for outdoor space became essential.

Opposite Café, courtyard and chapel to the left

Below First floor plan
Bottom Roof terrace of activity room

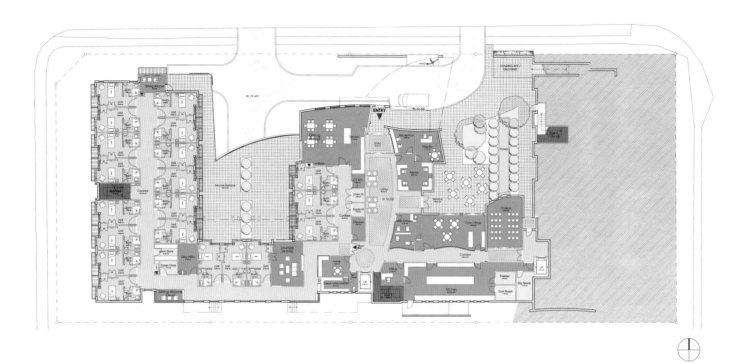

Other project information

'Inspired care' describes UnitingCare Ageing's person-centered approach to meeting the changing needs of their clients and residents in a holistic, compassionate way. Each person is honored as a unique individual, where services are tailored to that person's needs.

UnitingCare Ageing places great emphasis on the whole person—mind, body, and spirit—in their community and relationships. They strive to enable a rich and full lifestyle, respecting the person, their privacy, and their dignity throughout all aspects of their life. People receiving UnitedCare Ageing's services have the power to exercise choice and influence as much as possible over their life, their environment, and the services they receive.

The new facility 'Pacifica' was to offer a contemporary design of four community household accommodation clusters, each with its own color scheme, unique décor, and resident-driven vibe. Be welcoming to visiting friends and family within gracious and comfortable lounge areas equipped with a fireplace and large screen television, or in one of the more intimate sitting or reading areas or share a meal in the dining room. Each household offers a welcoming feel of home.

The architectural design of the building maximizes harmony with the surrounding natural environment and offers a stylish spacious lifestyle in a unique vertical design. The views from the rooftop terraces to the scenic surrounding hills will offer possibilities for outdoor entertaining, relaxation and recreation.

Environmental Sustainability & Energy Conservation

Passive Energy Conservation

The slender wings of the building footprint optimize natural light penetration into the plan depth and assist in natural cross-ventilation. The overall building form and plan provide a predominantly sunny northern orientation. Both roof and walls were insulated well in excess of minimum statutory energy conservation standards and all glazing utilizes performance e-glass to reduce thermal loss in winter and gain in summer. All north/east/west-facing openings were screened with horizontal louvered hoods or vertical screens.

High-level clerestory windows above the corridors are motorized to allow for natural light and airflow via a connection to the building management system (BMS).

First floor bedrooms and public areas will benefit from natural ventilation when outside air temperatures reach suitable levels. Roof water is collected in large underground storage tanks for re-use in the laundry and bathrooms. Triple-A rated faucet fixtures ensure efficient water usage.

Active Energy Saving Measures

The Building Management System (BMS) will be used to alternate between air conditioning mode and natural air mode. Heat pumps are used to generate hot water.

Advanced Technology

'Pacifica' provides its residents with in-room IT systems and associated security to support resident independence. As well as all necessary emergency, notification, and access facilities, the project utilizes the most up-to-date management care technology and provides computerized care stations discretely positioned throughout the residential areas to aid skilled staff with resident care management to enhance operational effectiveness.

Design & Philosophy of Care

The overall master plan that structured the project design, creating a collection of four communities based on the 'house' model, basically utilizes a floor for each 'house' and creates within the facility a collection of small warm domestic clusters that have all the features of a home-like environment. Within the 'house', a variety of smaller intimate sitting spaces away from the main living and dining areas provide further variety and interaction between residents and their guests. The control of space, color, and texture help define the public/private separation necessary to reinforce and make the domestic environment predominate over the back-of-house service facilities.

Integration of Residents with the Broader Community

The proximity of the 'Pacifica' site to the local town center offered opportunities to make the facility more open to the local community. Within the limits of ensuring a secure environment for the residents of Pacifica, a ground level welcoming café and garden terrace were incorporated into the design from an early stage. Given the steepness of the site and its relative smallness, most outdoor recreational space was created from secure roof terraces, which ensures a degree of openness not often found in aged care facilities.

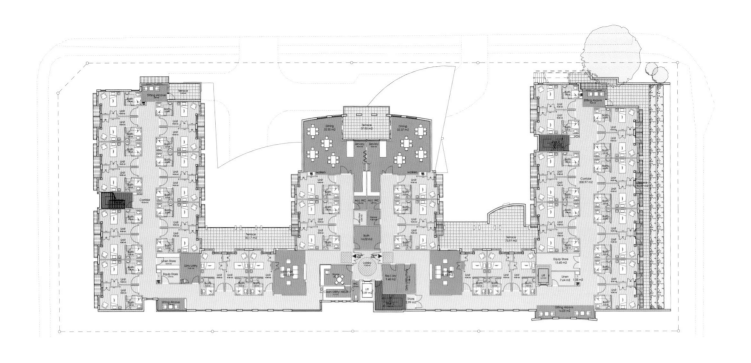

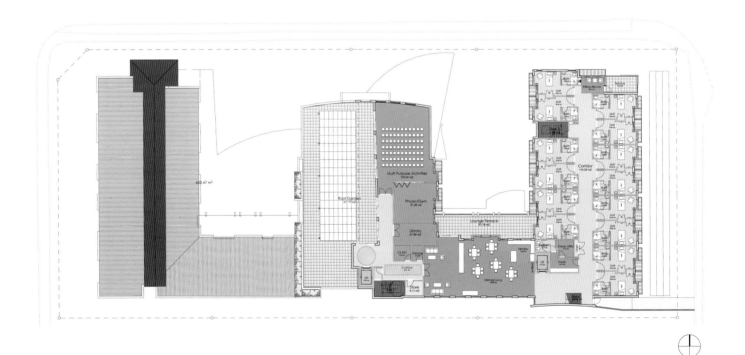

Staffing

Total number of staff at this project/facility 25

Number of management staff 5

Number of care staff (registered nursing and direct care staff) 13

Number of other staff (e.g. maintenance, housekeeping, food services) 4

Project Capacity and Numbers of Units

Special care for persons with dementia 20 beds

Skilled nursing care 86 beds (includes the dementia care above)

Kitchen (daily meals served) All meals to all residents from in-house central kitchen served to each 'house' and then served individually within the house.

Elder day care (clients) Day care available

Elder outreach (clients) 'Extended aged care at home' services available

Fitness/rehab/wellness (daily visits) Aged care therapy center, hairdresser, chapel, and library

Breakdown of Dementia Special Care Units

Studio/bed-sit units 20

Typical size per unit Dementia accommodation within the skilled nursing care units below

Opposite top Second floor plan

Opposite bottom Third floor plan

Above North east street corner

Breakdown of Skilled Nursing Care Units

Single occupancy rooms 86 ageing in place rooms (includes 20 dementia-specific rooms)

Typical size per unit 25m² and 37m²

Resident/Client Age

Current average age approximately 87 years old

Age upon entry approximately 85 years old

Resident/Client Fees and Funding

Entry fee or unit purchase Yes

Client monthly funding Private (out-of-pocket) pay

Public/Government funded

Public/Government subsidies (means-tested based on assets and/or income)

As is the trend with most aged care facilities, the more elderly clients (especially aged 85 or older) are occupying the beds as they generally have a higher level of care needs. There is a skew towards female residents who have longer life expectancy. Approximately 20 percent of the facility's residents are in need of dementia care.

As with the majority of Australian residential aged care facilities, most beds are supported by a Commonwealth Government subsidy. Currently this subsidy is paid to the facility as a 'licensed bed.' Prospective residents must first be assessed by a Government Aged Care Assessment Team (independent of any facility) to become eligible to take a room/bed in an aged care facility. As well as the subsidy from the government, facilities are permitted to charge residents a (refundable) bond on the facility's 'lower care' beds. Organizations such as UnitingCare often allow access to some approved residents to beds without payment of a bond.

Port Macquarie UnitingCare Ageing 'Mingaletta'

Port Macquarie, New South Wales, Australia

UnitingCare Ageing NSW.ACT (North Coast Region) / Campbell Luscombe Architects

Project Type Special Care Residence (for those with dementia), Skilled Nursing Care Residence

Site location Small Town

Site size 14,677 m²

Building footprint 3,635m²

Building area 7,225m²

Building cost $3,050/m²

Date completed February 2012

Photography Jeremy Rogers Photography

Owner's Statement

The project was one of two aged care facilities commissioned concurrently, approximately 90 kilometers apart on the mid-north coast of NSW. Crucial to the design is UnitingCare Ageing's commitment to creating a home-like environment that is full of domestic character and fosters a person-centered care approach. It was envisaged that this concept would look like a collection of individual communities within a residential care facility, with small warm community clusters that have all the features of a home-like environment. Service facilities such as serveries, kitchens, and pan rooms should be strategically positioned to not compromise the home-like environment and yet aim at servicing maximum numbers of residents.

As within a town concept, the community areas such as chapel, café, shop, hairdresser, and library should be in a central hub to create a feeling of adventure and outing for residents and located to provide the maximum number of residents ease of access. The residential facility design should allow residents to feel they are at home and have the ability to access all elements of service, with the independence and warmth which they currently enjoy in their everyday lives.

The architectural design of the building should maximize harmony with the surrounding natural environment and use all practicable efforts to enhance sustainability. The facility at the Port Macquarie site, 'Mingaletta,' was to accommodate 110 new single bed/ensuite resident rooms.

Right Covered drop-off is below awning of the building

Opposite Entry to Mingaletta

Architect's Statement

UnitingCare Ageing's strategy to satisfy the need for aged care services on the mid-north coast of NSW was, rather than providing one large facility, to instead develop two independent sites concurrently, one at Port Macquarie NSW, 300 kilometers north of Sydney, and a second, 90 kilometers further up the coast at Nambucca Heads. The design needed to respond carefully to UnitingCare Ageing's recently implemented Service and Care models. However, the particulars of the individual sites necessitated individual responses to each facility.

The design sought to embody the concept of 'normalcy,' to reflect a home setting rather than an institutional facility. Despite being quite a large building within its context, internally the layout discarded the 'healthcare' environment to provide a calm home-like ambiance. The separate resident wings, like the spokes of a wheel spreading from a 'hub,' break down the individual care units into 'houses.' Each house has its own legible 'front door' and entry, and its own domestic kitchen is reinforced by a strong linear hierarchy of privacy, from front door to bedroom.

The 'Mingaletta' site was relatively flat, but being bordered by a highway on one side and a major arterial road on the other, traffic noise was an issue and the site was at some distance from Port Macquarie town center. The design utilized the wings resulting from the care model to create restful landscaped interior courtyards.

Opposite Entry and drop-off to Mingaletta
Below First floor plan
Bottom Ground floor plan

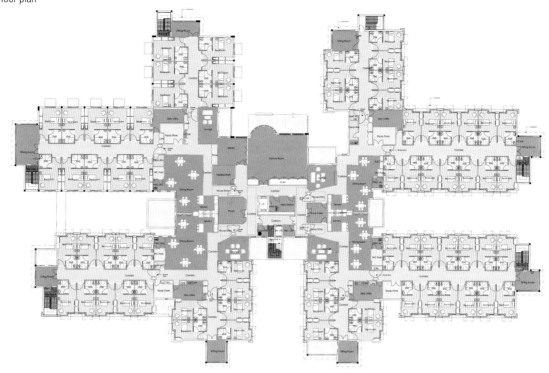

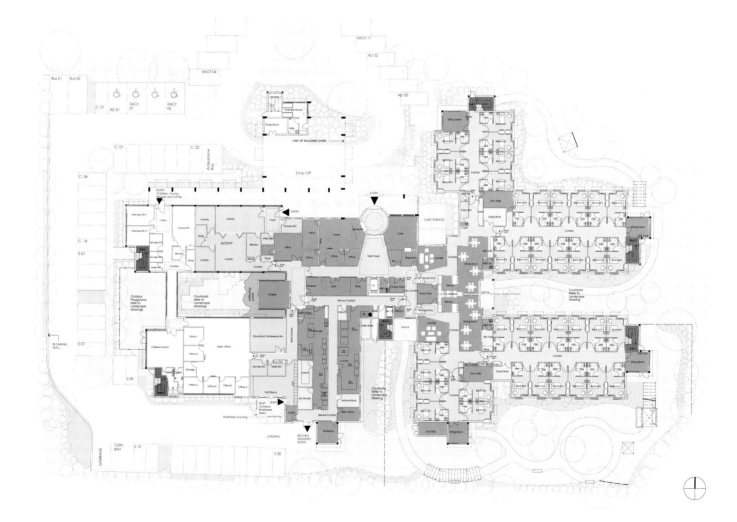

Client Goals and Design Team Solutions

1 Client goal: To develop the 'household' model of care.

Design team solution: The architectural resolution entailed the division of the 110 residential bedrooms into separate wings, each housing between 16 to 20 beds. Each 'house' wing (actually an L-shaped configuration to minimize corridor length) contained its own legible front door and private lobby space, a small sitting and dining area for each 'house,' a fully equipped domestic kitchen and a collection of additional small sitting/lounge areas which further break down the effect of the shortened corridors. The 'house' domestic kitchen, while functional in itself, was used as a servery for meals brought to the 'house' from the on-site central commercial kitchen. The necessary service areas associated with nursing care, utility rooms, nurses stations, additional toilets, among other facilities, are all discreetly located and are imperceptible to the ambiance of the domestic environment.

2 Client goal: The 'town concept' of residences and services.

Design team solution: Outside the residential 'houses,' the facility provides two distinct categories of support space. Firstly, the resident community spaces; therapy and consulting rooms, a hairdressing salon, a library, a chapel, and a café are generally concentrated and located adjacent to or off the main building entry to encourage the residents to leave their 'house' and create a feeling of an outing.

Secondly, the necessary back of house components, that include staff and education facilities, the commercial-sized kitchen and laundry that serve the entire facility have been located and are serviced from the rear and do not form part of the public and resident experience of the building.

Major Design Objectives and/or Project Challenges and the Related Responses

1 The home-like environment: To reinforce the perception of home, each resident should feel their space defined through their domestic surrounds. The major challenge to the residential aged care facility is that the necessarily large infrastructure needed to service the medical and residential needs of a great number of frail, elderly people in an economically viable manner, can so easily become institutional and hospital like. The solution largely disguises that infrastructure in support of the small scale and individual. As outlined above, as well as the creation of smaller residential clusters and the small intimate spaces it contains, even meals prepared in the central kitchen are brought to the house and served from the individual domestic kitchen.

2 Architectural character: Within the residential aged care sector, the current ageing population and their families are demanding a quality of environment and care that offers a sense of community, familiarity, dignity, and respect. They will demand to be securely integrated into the broader community in all tiers of seniors housing and care. By the nature of the size of this facility, it would inevitably be a large building within the surrounding small town suburban context. To sit comfortably within this context, the mass of the building has been broken down into legible parts, further reinforced by the use of a polychromatic brick selection. The building presents a strong identity of entry and approach, but each part breaks further down to ultimately also identify each individual room with a contemporary bay window arrangement.

3 Maximise the ESD potential of the development: See the 'Environmental Sustainability & Energy Conservation' section below.

Right Collection of small sitting areas terminating a corridor

Opposite top left Timber entry floor

Opposite top right Room dividers break up larger spaces

Opposite bottom Domestic 'living rooms' to each house

Unique Context

The project's client, a 'not for profit' organization, is a division of a major church, and is one of Australia's largest providers of aged care services. The client prides itself on its care models and the research it undertakes on international trends in aged services and is often at the forefront of aged care provision in Australia.

Port Macquarie is a medium-sized coastal town on the mid-north coast of NSW, approximately 300 kilometers north of Sydney. The site is a residual parcel of land from a large adjacent church. The site is wedge shaped, formed by the intersection of a small country highway and a local arterial road. The surrounding context is generally suburban, but with other seniors and aged care developments opposite the site. While the site area was generous, the client envisaged maximizing the overall site potential by locating the new facility with the intention of developing future seniors housing on the remainder of the unutilized area. The site is within the suburban fringe of the town and some distance from community services and needed to be self-sufficient socially. Being on the western town fringe, however, the site offered some proximity to the natural bushland that surrounds the suburb area.

Other Project Information

'Inspired care' describes UnitingCare Ageing's person-centered approach to meeting the changing needs of their clients and residents in a holistic, compassionate way. Each person is honored as a unique individual where services are tailored to that person's needs.

UnitingCare Ageing places great emphasis on the whole person—mind, body, and spirit—in their community and relationships. They strive to enable a rich and full lifestyle, respecting the person, their privacy and their dignity throughout all aspects of their life. People receiving UCA's services have the power to exercise choice and influence as much as possible over their life, their environment, and the services they receive.

Early in the design phase, the client, UnitingCare Ageing, formed an association with another division of the church. This group, unrelated to aged care, focused on community counselling and support for families and children. It was decided to house the local branch of this support organization within the new building. The client had also decided as an adjunct to its aged care accommodation, to provide for seniors' day care. Each of these services, while often sharing some facilities and staff with the main facility, were required to present publically as individual and separate ground level addresses to that of the new aged care facility.

Environmental Sustainability & Energy Conservation

Passive Energy Conservation

The slender wings of the building footprint optimize natural light penetration into the plan depth and assist in natural cross-ventilation. The overall building form and plan reduce the extent of the west-facing façade and provide a predominantly northern orientation.

Both roof and walls were insulated well in excess of minimum statutory energy conservation standards and all glazing utilized performance e-glass to reduce thermal loss in winter and gain in summer. All north-facing openings were screened with horizontal louvered hoods or vertical screens.

High-level south-facing clerestory windows above the corridors are motorized to allow for natural light and air flow via a connection to the building management system (BMS). First floor bedrooms and public areas will benefit from natural ventilation when outside air temperatures reach suitable levels. On the ground floor, full height operable louvered windows allow for cross-ventilation to the office and child care areas. Roof water is collected in large underground storage tanks for re-use in the laundry and bathrooms. Triple-A rated faucet fixtures ensure efficient water usage.

Active Energy Saving Measures

The Building Management System (BMS) will be used to alternate between air conditioning mode and natural air mode. Heat pumps are used to generate hot water. The north-facing angled high light roof elements will allow for the installation of photo-voltaic cell panels.

Advanced Technology

'Mingaletta' provides its residents with in-room IT systems and associated security to support resident independence. As well as all necessary emergency, notification and access facilities, the project utilizes the most up-to-date management care technology and provides computerized care stations discretely positioned throughout the residential areas to aid skilled staff with resident care management to enhance operational effectiveness.

Design & Philosophy of Care

The overall masterplan of 'hub and spoke' that structured the project design into a collection of six communities based on the 'house' model creates within the facility a collection of small warm domestic clusters that have all the features of a home-like environment. Within the 'house,' a variety of smaller intimate sitting spaces away from the main living and dining areas provide further variety and interaction between residents and their guests. The control of space, color, and texture help define the public/private separation necessary to reinforce and make the domestic environment prevail over the back of house service facilities.

Integration of Residents with the Broader Community

As noted above, 'Mingaletta' houses a seniors' day care center that provides relief services to full time carers in the surrounding community, as well as stimulation and social interaction for those in its care. While the family and child support counselling services housed within the building do not necessarily bring interaction to the facility's residents, the site is enlivened by the greater flow of people, and the facilities such as the café and the chapel are available to all who use the site.

Staffing

Total number of staff at this project/facility 32

Number of management staff 7

Number of care staff (registered nursing and direct care staff) 16

Number of other staff (e.g. maintenance, housekeeping, food services) 6

Project Capacity and Numbers of Units

Special care for persons with dementia 19 beds

The design permits an adjacent wing of 20 beds to be converted to dementia care in the future.

Skilled nursing care (beds) 110 (includes the dementia care beds above)

Kitchen (daily meals served) All meals to all residents from in-house central kitchen served to each 'house' and then served individually within the house.

Elder day care (clients) Yes, with separate entry from the main facility

Elder outreach (clients) 'Extended aged care at home' services available

Fitness/rehab/wellness (daily visits) Aged care therapy center, café, hairdresser, chapel, and library

Breakdown of Dementia Special Care Units

Studio/bed-sit units 19 (+)

Typical size per unit *see below

* Dementia accommodation within the skilled nursing care units below.

Breakdown of Skilled Nursing Care Units

One bed/single occupancy rooms 110 ageing in place rooms (includes 19 dementia-specific rooms)

Typical size per room 25m² and 30m²

Resident/Client Age

Current average age approximately 87 years old

Age upon entry approximately 85 years old

Resident/Client Fees and Funding

Entry fee Yes

Client Monthly Funding Private (out-of-pocket) pay

Public/Government funded

Public/Government subsidies (means tested based on assets and/or income)

As is the trend with most aged care facilities, the more elderly clients (especially aged 85 or more) are occupying the beds as they generally have higher levels of care needs. There is a bias towards female residents who have longer life expectancies. Approximately 20 per cent of the facility's residents are in need of dementia care. The design of 'Mingaletta' allows for the doubling of the dementia-specific resident figure in the future.

As with the majority of Australian residential aged care facilities, most beds are supported by a Commonwealth Government subsidy. Currently this subsidy is paid to the facility as a 'licensed bed.' Prospective residents must first be assessed by a Government Aged Care Assessment Team (independent of any facility) to become eligible to take a room/bed in an aged care facility. As well as the subsidy from the government, facilities are permitted to charge residents a (refundable) bond on the facility's 'lower care' beds. Organizations such as UnitingCare often allow access to some approved residents to beds without payment of a bond.

Rincon del Rio Senior Living

South Nevada County, California, USA
Young Enterprises / McCamant and Durrett Architects

Project type Active Senior/
Independent Living Residence,
Assisted Living/Hostel Residence,
Community-Based Services,
Multi-Level Care/Continuing Care
Retirement Communities, Special
Care Residence (for those with
dementia), Senior Cohousing
Community

Site location Rural

Site size 87 hectares

Building footprint 1,520m²

Building area 49,490m², of which
37,840m² residential

Total building cost US$80 million

Building cost US$1,615/m²

Date completed Scheduled for 2016

Photography Charles Durrett

Owner's Statement

Rincon del Rio is a 345-unit senior living complex for approximately 450 residents in South Nevada County. Located on 86 hectares along the Bear River, the project includes a variety of residential unit types in a campus setting that also includes community support services, recreational opportunities, farmland, and open space.

The Rincon Del Rio Continuing Care Retirement Community (CCRC), incorporating commercial space, private dwellings, and a cohousing community, will be a model sustainable community by drastically curtailing both social isolation and carbon emissions of its senior residents. This vibrant mixed-use neighborhood is clustered to preserve 80 per cent of the site as open space and to ensure that all 345 residential units are walkable to the 5,575-square meter Village Center. Seniors will have full access to gourmet dining, recreation, shops, and medical facilities without needing to drive.

All Rincon's homes will be at least 80 per cent solar powered, 40 per cent more efficient than California State Energy regulations Title 24, and the first in the County to use reclaimed water from the local water treatment plant. All these measures equate to an approximately 60 per cent smaller carbon footprint and significantly lower utility bills for every resident. A central event green, fitness/aquatic centers, organic vegetable gardens, 10-hectare working farm and extensive walking trails encourage an active lifestyle, while gathering areas, community projects, and group activities will result in a neighborhood where seniors age successfully by becoming more social, active, and sustainable.

Right Rendering of the view from the front porch of a cottage unit

Opposite Rincon del Rio site plan

134

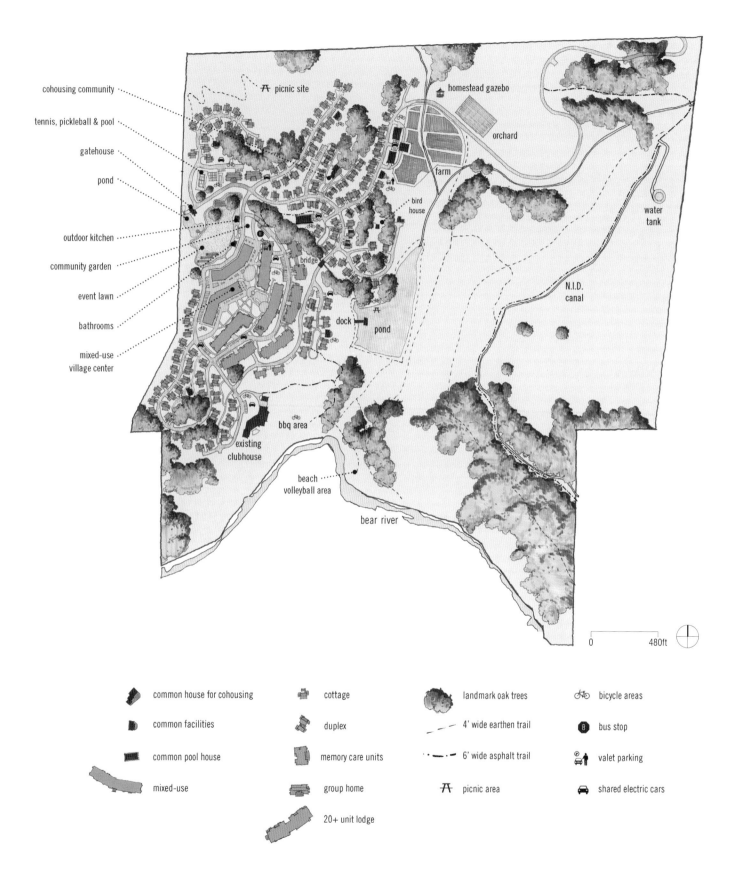

cohousing community
tennis, pickleball & pool
gatehouse
pond
outdoor kitchen
community garden
event lawn
bathrooms
mixed-use
village center

picnic site
homestead gazebo
orchard
farm
bird
house
bridge
N.I.D.
canal
water
tank
dock
pond
bbq area
existing
clubhouse
beach
volleyball area
bear river

0   480ft

common house for cohousing   cottage   landmark oak trees   bicycle areas

common facilities   duplex   4' wide earthen trail   bus stop

common pool house   memory care units   6' wide asphalt trail   valet parking

mixed-use   group home   picnic area   shared electric cars

20+ unit lodge

Architect's Statement

Rincon del Rio is located on 86 hectares along the Bear River in South Nevada County. The project proposes a Senior Living Retirement Community designed to have a small-town feel. Amenities and services are offered throughout the village, including a hair salon, spa rooms, dining facilities, doctor's offices, and more. Also part of the development is a 20-unit cohousing community, enhancing the village setting.

The traditional village setting offers seniors a variety of housing and experiences, including: cottages, duplexes, group homes, lodges, and village center residential units. The lodge and village units both provide independent living as well as assisted living options.

Services provided are: housekeeping, massage, meals (including special diet services), arranged transportation, emergency help, medical assistance, and personal assistants.

As the first village model CCRC in the USA, Rincon del Rio is designed to be extremely inviting to families and to accommodate extended stays. Too many CCRCs disinvite family by virtue of the smells, mono-use, and how boring it is, especially for young children, teenagers, and young adults. Rincon is designed so that a teenager can come and visit his or her grandparent for 30 minutes, go and do something else interesting, and then come back while mum and dad are still there.

Above Rendering of the village walkway located at the center of the project
Opposite top Lodge floor plan, which has units designed for assisted living
Opposite bottom Duplex unit floor plan

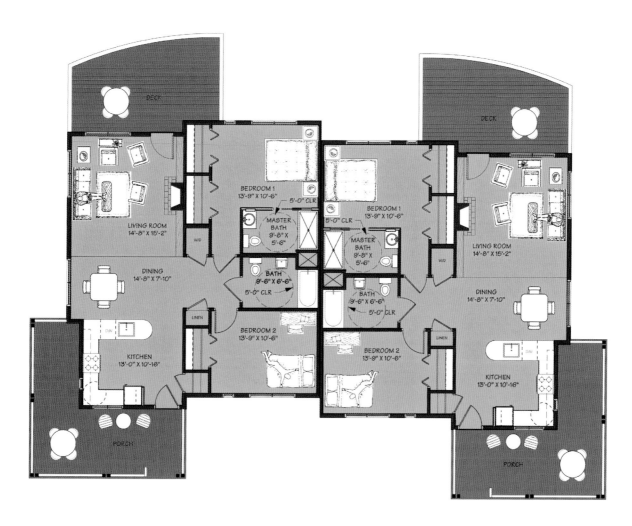

Client Goals and Design Team Solutions

1 Client Goal: Retain the natural and rural feel of the site.

Design team solution: The huge array of outdoor environments, from the front porch, the back deck, the paths, the walkways, the bridges, the farm, the pond, the river, the open space, and the common terraces, create the feeling of "living outside." These all allow for seniors to live outside, while also having a beautiful abode.

2 Client Goal: Village-like development.

Design team solution: By retaining the rural feel of the site, the buildings were clustered together to create a village-like feel. The community is dense for people to have a casual encounter in town and invite them for a hike beyond.

3 Client Goal: A sense of community.

Design team solution: The goal of the residence is to foster a community. Living together is the right thing and when people support each other, they can minimize "care"—that is, nursing homes and institutionalized care.

Major Design Objectives and/or Project Challenges and the Related Responses

1 Retaining a rural setting: The clustered design retains the rural setting that seniors value in Nevada County. The clustered design only takes up 20 per cent of the site, leaving 80 per cent to be natural open space.

2 Creating appropriate senior housing in Nevada County: 74 per cent of current Nevada County seniors that want to be surrounded by nature and prefer to live outside of town. 79 per cent want homes designed so they can age in place and stay in Nevada County. Everything is built using universal design for "easy living."

3 Garden Space: The garden is a major part of the site design. Not only will residents have access to raised beds for personal gardening, but they will also be able to hold farmers' markets within the community. This gets seniors moving, outside working and staying young.

Opposite top Rendering of the lodge containing mostly residential units
Opposite bottom Rendering of a cluster of duplex units
Above Front elevation of a mixed-use building containing retail and residences

Unique Context

The Rincon del Rio site is in a pastoral setting, with verdant foliage, scenic vistas, ponds, and a serene atmosphere. It enhances these positive attributes with walking trails, contemplation areas, groomed, picturesque landscaping, and community gardens. The buildings are clustered on the western 14 hectares, preserving the natural beauty and ecosystems of the rest of the site. For a property to be extraordinary, it has to give people the impetus to be something they might not have been without experiencing that setting. That's the uniqueness of Rincon del Rio. It offers quality and choices regarding housing and services as you age. The location is a treasure—really magic.

The objective is to create unique environments that attract new friends from throughout the village and surrounding neighborhoods. The goal is to defeat inactivity, boredom, isolation, and depression. With everything so close at hand, and with such a variety of interests and platforms encouraging exploration and well being, success is just a step outside the front door.

Increasingly, the future community is aware of the relevance of green, sustainable housing and neighborhood practices that encourage health, safety, and happiness throughout life. Rincon del Rio incorporates these values within the context of senior housing.

Environmental Sustainability & Energy Conservation

Rincon del Rio will have a 60 per cent reduction of total emissions than a normal development of the same size. This includes vehicle emissions reducing by 55 per cent due to pedestrian-oriented development and use of alternative vehicles; electricity reduction of 60 per cent with the help of solar panels; general site reduction of emissions by 60 per cent due to solar hot water and electric garden equipment; and finally a 65 per cent reduction of water and waste with the integration of recycling and compost services as well as efficient water appliances and reuse of grey water for irrigation.

Advanced Technology

The community will integrate solar hot water heating supplied from the roof of each residential building. 90 per cent of the total household gas use is for water and space heating. These solar hot water systems will assist gas boilers by more than 50 per cent.

The site will also have alternative modes of transportation for the residents to get around in. These will include bikes, electric-assisted bikes, electric carts, electric jitneys, hybrid cars, and hybrid shuttles. Each household will have a touch screen transit locator, which assists with coordinating rides and many other cooperative possibilities, for instance "Who wants to go for a walk at 10am?"

Design & Philosophy of Care

Rincon del Rio CCRC has various options for housing within the community. There are assisted-living units within the community—57 in total. These units provide the extra care that some may need. The buildings with assisted living units are designed to have a lobby with receptionist, a sitting area for residents to wait for rides or friends, a nurse's office for consultants and routine visits, space for visiting doctors, and a spa for relaxing and assisted bathing.

Rincon del Rio assigns each resident a Certified Case Manager (CCM) to co-ordinate home service for any range of ADL needs or requests. Disability or on-going management of chronic conditions such as diabetes or cancer require the support of a whole home care team and includes nursing, therapies and necessary equipment and supplies—all co-ordinated by a CCM.

Integration of Residents with the Broader Community

The heart of the community is the Village Center, a mixed-use neighborhood where residents and visitors of all ages will congregate. Facing the central plaza are shops, including a bakery, the main restaurant, a sports bar/grill, a hardware store, hair and beauty salon, and professional offices as well as a rose garden, bandstand, kids' area, and other features that elders, adult children, and grandchildren alike will enjoy.

The site will have a 25-acre vegetable garden and fruit orchard; the wider population will be invited to participate with classes and real farmers. Farming is in the air and after the age of 60, growing tomatoes is a bit of a competitive sport. Rincon makes that fun.

Staffing

Total number of staff at the facility 55

Number of management staff 20

Number of care staff (registered nursing and direct care staff) 20

Direct care hours per day per client up to 8 (no nursing care)

Number of other staff (e.g. maintenance, housekeeping, food services) 20

Project Capacity and Numbers of Units

Independent living apartments 96

Independent living cottages/villas 155

Assisted living/hostel care 57

Special care for persons with dementia 8

Skilled nursing care 8

Group houses 5 houses of 345m², each containing 6 bedrooms and 7 bathrooms

Breakdown of Independent Living Units

Two bedroom units 251
Typical size per unit 99m²

Breakdown of Assisted Living/Hostel Care Units

Two bedroom units 57
Typical size per unit 84m²

Breakdown of Dementia Special Care Units

Two bedroom units 8
Typical size per unit 84m²

Breakdown of Skilled Nursing Care Units

Two bedroom units 8
Typical size per unit 84m²

Resident/Client Age

Average age upon entry between 55 and 90 years

Resident/Client Fees and Funding

Entry fee or unit purchase Yes

Client Monthly Funding Private (out-of-pocket) pay

The residents of Rincon del Rio Senior Living are committed to living an independent lifestyle while being surrounded by friends, amenities, services, and outdoor activities. Purely a CCRC, the Village allows the residents to live with the people they want to. Anybody is welcome to live in Rincon, as long as they want to be part of a community. Ranging from 55 to 90 years old, the residents are and have been very active members of the larger community. Many of them seek a caring, giving and co-operative environment for themselves and the caregivers.

The staffing strategy for Rincon del Rio is to build as much community as possible in order to keep staffing levels down. The goal is to institutionalize sharing, for example, carpooling and other activities.

Top left View from the birdhouse ,which is ADA accessible
Top right Meandering path leading to the birdhouse

Silver Sage Senior Cohousing

Boulder, Colorado, USA

Silver Sage Cohousing LCC / McCamant & Durrett Architects

Project type Active Senior/
Independent Living Residence,
Community-Based Services,
Senior Cohousing

Site location Urban

Site size 0.34 hectares

Building footprint 1,520m²

Building area 2,610m²

Total building cost US$4 million

Building cost US$1,560/m²

Date completed 2009

Photography Charles Durrett

Owner's Statement

Silver Sage Cohousing is the third senior cohousing community in the United States consisting of three 2-story buildings with 16 dwelling units, a common house, an arts and crafts buildings, garages, and carports situated around the common terrace and a large garden court.

Silver Sage allows seniors to age-in-place and prevents institutionalized care. The communities are unique in their extensive use of common facilities and—more importantly—in that they are organized, planned, and managed by the residents themselves. Yet cohousing is distinctive in that each family or household has a separate dwelling and chooses how much he or she wants to participate in community activities.

At Silver Sage, the residents like to call themselves empty-nesters, active adults, near-seniors, human beings, but most of all members of a community. The group was determined to create a community that supports each resident and where the members expect to live comfortably for the balance of their lives. Their purpose is "Spiritual Eldering: nurturing and encouraging of people's desires to keep learning, growing, and participating."

The group wanted a place that would support these desires. By integrating community garden space, outdoor balconies and walkways, a central staircase, common terrace, shared meals, proximity to downtown Boulder, and location within the Holiday Neighborhood, which is new and very eclectic; the residents are able to age in place successfully. All these elements are meant to support meaningful interaction and rejuvenating solitude, as well as promote a place for connection where the residents are inspired to learn, create, and share with each other.

Right Silver Sage Senior Cohousing's common terrace at night

Opposite The cohousing from the street shows large overhangs to shade the building from the sun.

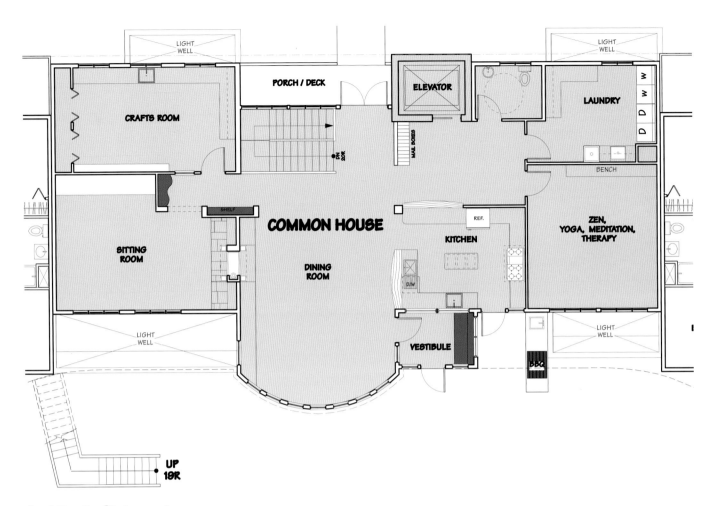

Labels within floor plan: LIGHT WELL, PORCH / DECK, ELEVATOR, LIGHT WELL, LAUNDRY, CRAFTS ROOM, W, W, D, D, BENCH, MAIL BOXES, DN 20R, SHELF, COMMON HOUSE, REF., ZEN, YOGA, MEDITATION, THERAPY, SITTING ROOM, KITCHEN, DINING ROOM, D/W, LIGHT WELL, LIGHT WELL, VESTIBULE, BBQ, UP 18R

Architect's Statement

Silver Sage Senior Cohousing, also known as Silver Sage Village, is the third senior cohousing in the United States. Thoughtfully designed by the residents themselves, the intention was to design a place that has soul. And the only way that was going to be accomplished was to work directly with the people who planned to live there. Inspired by *Senior Cohousing: A Community Approach to Independent Living*, the residents tried to adhere to the participatory design process laid out there.

The community is on 0.34 hectares located in the Holiday Neighborhood in Boulder, Colorado. The urban site allows the residents to walk downtown easily, giving access to restaurants, shops, public transportation, and more.

The community is made up of 16 condominiums—each containing its own kitchen, living room, dining room, and bathrooms. A common house is at the center of the Village, which supplements the private houses with facilities including a public dining room and kitchen, sitting room, crafts room, media room, library, guest rooms, and storage.

A large garden court is at the center, where residents have planted their own vegetables, flowers, and trees. The court, along with extensive public decks, creates substantial open space in the dense urban neighborhood.

Above Common house floor plan
Opposite top The view from the common balcony
Opposite bottom The residents enjoying common dinner on the terrace

Client Goals and Design Team Solutions

1 Client Goal: Nourish body and soul.

Design team solution: The residents desired a community where they could nourish body and soul with good food, good health, and good company. The common house and terrace allow the residents to share meals with their friends.

2 Client Goal: Stylish living.

Design team solution: The residents were included in the design process from the very beginning. This meant they had input on every decision made and were able to shape the spaces the way they wanted them and experience stylish living with thoughtfully designed interiors.

3 Client Goal: Inviting outdoor spaces.

Design team solution: The group felt strongly about sharing inviting outdoor spaces such as gardens, courtyards, decks, patios, and views. The large outdoor space in the center of the project houses garden space and each courtyard, deck, and patio look out into this open space.

Major Design Objectives and/or Project Challenges and the Related Responses

1 Social community: The main goal for Silver Sage Village was to create a social community that supports each resident. Every aspect of the community promotes engagement and co-operation with other residents.

2 Create a focal point: The common house and terrace are at the center of the project. This creates a focal point that serves as a link with Wild Sage Cohousing, located directly across the street. Wild Sage is the first senior cohousing community, so it was important for Silver Sage to implement this connection.

3 Strong edges: The private houses flank the common house and set strong edges for the site. Each house has a patio offering views both into the site and out towards the neighborhood. The porches also engage the streets and neighbors, lending a friendly face to the public side of the project.

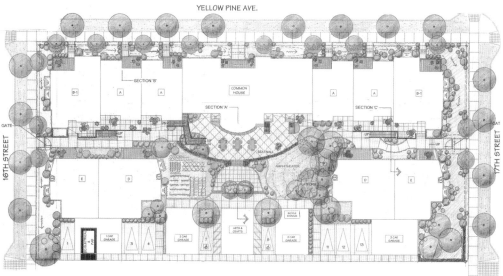

YELLOW PINE AVE.

Opposite top left Back yard of a private house unit

Opposite top right An entry gate located on both the East and West sides of the site

Opposite bottom View of the common house terrace

Above View of the common garden court

Left Landscape site plan

Unique Context

At Silver Sage, neighbors of different ages and backgrounds often become friends. The small-scale (16-unit) participatory senior cohousing, consisting primarily of adults over the age of 50, actively built their community. It is an exceptionally vibrant, visionary, and openhearted place to live, with amenities close at hand, which combines the privacy of owning your own home with the enjoyment of a shared community. Care at Silver Sage is organic, neighbors caring for neighbors, and hired in when necessary.

Within walking distance, residents can find coffee shops, restaurants, bars, a bank, a pizzeria, a bakery, bike shop, local gym, grocery store, and a lovely park. Just five minutes away is downtown Boulder, the Pearl Street pedestrian mall, and the University of Colorado Boulder, which holds events open to the public.

Silver Sage is located close to national parks and mountains for skiing, creating a community that is a true outdoor paradise for active adults. It recently earned a National Association of Home Builders (NAHB) Silver Award for best of 50+ Housing in 2008.

Environmental Sustainability & Energy Conservation

There are two design features in Silver Sage that really promote cohousing's ability to be environmentally sustainable and energy conservative. Putting washers and dryers into individual units can lead to an extensive amount of energy use, not to mention excessive water use. By putting only one laundry facility in the community, located in the common house, the residents are encouraged to use the facility, catch up with a friend, and conserve energy and water all at once.

The other feature is a central recycling and garbage station. As has been claimed in the architect's office, the "Temple to Recycling" promotes recycling and gets the residents to think. Most importantly, it works. At Quayside Cohousing in North Vancouver, British Columbia, the 18-unit community generates the same amount of solid waste as the single-family home next door. Silver Sage achieves close to the same.

Advanced Technology

The design of Silver Sage does not pride itself on using advanced technology, but rather integrates smart and simple moves to make for the most energy efficient building that is easy to maintain. These include in-floor radiant hydronic heat for private house interiors, a water catchment pond for landscape irrigation, high fly-ash concrete for patios, blown-in cellulose insulation for optimum R-values, photovoltaic panels to support electrical loads, and pervious hardscape materials for slow water infiltration. Energy conservation features include radiant barriers on the roof, perimeter foundation insulation, and light-colored roofs. Many features on the roof and in the walls (the envelope) are reminiscent of the passive house.

Design & Philosophy of Care

Even though this resident group likes to be described as empty-nesters, active adults, or near-seniors, they do understand that care may be needed at some point in their future. Although there are no designated locations for caregivers, the common house offers two rooms for guests and/or caregivers. The units also range from two to three bedrooms, allowing a caregiver to move in with a resident once more care is necessary. Silver Sage is senior co-care without the institution.

Integration of Residents with the Broader Community

NoBo (North Boulder) was recently selected as one of the ten finalists in the "Live Work Play 2011"—the Denver Regional Council of Governments' awards program celebrating great places and livable communities in the Denver region. In a distinctly mixed-use neighborhood, people and businesses blend together, creating a sense of place that attracts people of all incomes and ages to live, work, and play.

Step out the door of Silver Sage Village into a well-planned neighborhood where you can wander past artist studios and galleries along the pedestrian walkway. You'll be within walking distance to public transportation linking you to every part of the city and beyond. All residents of the Holiday Homeowners Association have Ecopasses that provide free bus transport around town, to Denver, other cities, and to Denver International Airport.

Opposite top Interior of the common house dining room and kitchen
Opposite bottom Residents enjoying the sitting room in the common house

Top Residents going for a group bike ride

Above A resident gardening

Middle right Residents doing landscaping work in common garden court

Right Another resident gardening

Opposite Residents having common house dinner on the terrace

Staffing

Total number of staff at this facility None at present, but they are designed to welcome a caregiver at a later date

Number of management staff Silver Sage is completely self-managed

Number of care staff (registered nursing and direct care staff) None, but they are designed to welcome a caregiver a later date

Direct care hours per day per client Currently none, except for neighbors

Number of other staff (e.g. maintenance, housekeeping, food services) Self-performed, or they hire help, like a naturally occurring retirement community

Project Capacity and Numbers of Units

Independent living apartments 16

Breakdown of Independent Living Units

Two bedroom units 16
Typical size per unit 144m²

Resident/Client Age

Current average age 70 years old
Average age upon entry 65 years old

Resident/Client Fees and Funding

Entry fee Yes ($125,000 to $750,000)

Client Monthly Funding Private (out-of-pocket) pay

The residents of Silver Sage are from all over the United States. Some grew up in Colorado, but have worked in other states for most of their adult lives. All of the residents were interested in living in a community with other people of similar age, likes, hobbies, and beliefs. It allows them to be active, enjoy the outdoors, and reside in a place they can truly call their own.

There are no staff at Silver Sage Senior Cohousing. The community is self-managed, where the residents rely on each other and neighbors for any other support. However, the cohousing was designed to accommodate caregivers at any given time.

The Solana at Cinco Ranch

Katy, Texas, USA

Formation Development Group / **three**: living architecture

Project type Active Senior/
Independent Living Residence,
Assisted Living/Hostel Residence,
Multi-Level Care/Continuing Care
Retirement Communities

Site location Suburban

Site size 2 hectares

Building footprint 3,725m²

Building area 18,195m²

Total building cost US$23,463,580

Building cost US$1,292/m²

Date completed August 2009

Photography Michael Wilson

Owner's Statement

As the initial venture of Formation Development Group, the relatively small and restricted site needed to provide maximum potential. The new community needed to compete with and exceed nearby competition. Individual residences needed to be luxurious, specifically with large balconies, bedrooms, and storage spaces. Common spaces were designed with a unique program, including multiple dining venues and distinct lounge areas, along with more typical residential spaces. The exterior of the project, while needing to conform to Cinco Ranch extensive design guidelines, needed to be distinguished, welcoming, and easily identifiable as the new "Solana" brand.

Below Entry view from Cinco Ranch Boulevard
Opposite The gallery

152

Architect's Statement

Located in a growing suburban community of Cinco Ranch, every square inch of the site is utilized—from a compact organization of independent living and assisted living residences, Commons, and a series of outdoor courts that provide activities from dining to bocce, to a resort pool and water feature. Due to budget restraints, all parking was required to be on-grade. Independent living residence designs include small 'bonus' spaces, which may be used as media rooms, dining, office, or study and have been found to be very popular with residents.

Resident corridor lengths are kept to a minimum and alcove areas provide furnishing tableaus that can be removed, should residents need space for motorized scooter storage. Cinco Ranch required a specific palette of exterior materials, from which a 'Texas Urban' style was crafted. Signature architectural forms highlight the building form, including a rotunda and tower, which relates to other prominent tower features nearby. Both the rotunda and tower elements found at The Solana at Cinco Ranch have been repeated on subsequent Solana projects nationwide.

Above Assisted Living lounge
Opposite Assisted Living dining

Client Goals and Design Team Solutions

1 **Client Goal:** Create a Solana signature look.

Design team solution: Along with the easily identifiable rotunda and tower elements on the exterior, The Solana set a benchmark for openness and transparency to the outdoors, which is apparent from the moment one enters the community. Great expanses of glass and views to lushly landscaped courts create a sense of welcome and an ease of orientation in the building and on campus.

2 **Client Goal:** Create Solana signature residences.

Design team solution: While the sizes of each residence are standard to nearby competition, prospective residents are 'sold' because the spaces seem much bigger than they are. Larger ceiling heights in ground floor residences, larger windows and exterior doors (and transoms), and the generous response to the need for more storage are greatly appreciated by residents.

3 **Client Goal:** Maximize the site!

Design team solution: The compact and efficient configuration of the site allows for more residences, while limiting walking distances. Special unique residences were placed within the tower and rotunda forms.

Major Design Objectives and/or Project Challenges and the Related Responses

1 **Building in a tight space:** When construction commenced, the site was set in the middle of undeveloped plats. The design team was challenged and questioned about the seemingly tight sizes of interior courtyards and open spaces. As the building rose, it was found that the court areas were very comfortable and welcoming, even for four-story structures.

In subsequent projects for Formation Development Group and The Solana brand, the architect is further testing the character of interior courts to allow for greater efficiency and maximum development, while maintaining a pleasant outdoor environment.

2 **Signature design elements:** On the interior and exterior, signature design elements were evaluated and deemed highly successful. Exterior rotunda and tower elements are repeated on Solana projects around the country, as are residential corridor alcoves that may be used for resident motorized scooter storage.

Unique Context

Along with limiting travel distance between resident units and dining and other common amenities, it was important to limit travel distance between resident units and parking. Since the community attracted a younger group of seniors, most residents had at least one vehicle per household. The architect's hope is that since the Cinco Ranch area is expanding with retail, restaurants, services, and other attractive amenities, most residents will abandon their vehicles in favor of an energetic pedestrian neighborhood.

Opposite Bistro dining
Above Independent Living apartment

Project Capacity and Numbers of Units

Independent living apartments 126

Assisted living/hostel care 32

Kitchen (daily meals served) 250

Elder outreach (clients) 75

Fitness/rehab/wellness (daily visits) 50

Pool(s) and related areas (daily visits) 50

Breakdown of Independent Living Units

One bedroom units 86
Typical size per unit 72m^2

Two bedroom units 36
Typical size per unit 98m^2

Two bedroom plus units 4
Typical size per unit 113m^2

Breakdown of Assisted Living/Hostel Care Units

Studio/bed-sit units 22
Typical size per unit 33m^2

One bedroom units 8
Typical size per unit 45m^2

Two bedroom units 2
Typical size per unit 54m^2

Resident/Client Fees and Funding

Entry fee or unit purchase Yes

Client Monthly Funding Private (out-of-pocket) pay

Left Independent Living dining court and pool
Above Independent Living activity court

Stillwater Senior Cohousing

Stillwater, Oklahoma, USA
Stillwater Senior Cohousing LLC / McCamant & Durrett Architects

Project type Active Senior/
Independent Living Residence,
Community-Based Services, Special
Feature Project, Senior Cohousing

Site location Small town

Site size 3 hectares

Building footprint 2,575m²

Building area 2,575m²

Total building cost US$3.3 million

Building cost US$1,291/m²

Date completed 2012

Photography Pat Darlington and
Charles Durrett (page 160)

Owner's Statement

Stillwater Cohousing, also known as Oakcreek, consists of 24 dwelling units, clustered into three 8-unit pods, and the renovated common house situated along generous open space. Oakcreek allows seniors to age-in-place and prevents institutionalized care. The communities are unique in their extensive use of common facilities and—more importantly—in that they are organized, planned, and managed by the residents themselves. Yet cohousing is distinctive in that each family or household has a separate dwelling and chooses how much he or she wants to participate in community activities.

The project was started by Pat Darlington who, after attending a week long seminar called "Ageing Successfully" held in Nevada City, California, decided that community, and living proximate to others who wanted to support each other, was the way to go. Oakcreek is a "senior cohousing" community in Stillwater, Oklahoma that was planned and developed by the residents themselves—a group of active older Oklahomans aged between 55 and 85 who wanted to take control of their future and age-in-place among neighbors and friends, not in a nursing home.

Not only does Oakcreek Community provide a friendly, caring environment for seniors, it also provides them with sufficient independence and privacy. The residents have the option to socialize, attend common meals cooked by their neighbors, and participate in other activities in a 325-square meter shared common house. Cohousing is designed so that residents have as much privacy as desired and as much community as desired.

Right The existing building on site that was renovated into the common house

Opposite top Rendering of the walkway between private houses

Opposite bottom Residents enjoying their common house

Private Units

Common House

Private Units

NORTH HUSBAND STREET

Architect's Statement

First is the concept of participatory process. The homeowners of Oakcreek helped plan, organize, and design their own neighborhood. Working from a common vision and well-articulated values, they collaborated with the architect to create the physical environment that supports their vision of "aging in place in this community of Stillwater."

Second, the physical design promotes and supports a strong sense of community. There are extensive common facilities, which serve as an integral part of the community and supplement smaller, but complete private homes. The dining area in the common house will be large enough to accommodate all the homeowners and guests, as some

common meals and gatherings are an essential part of community life. The outdoor terrace, common grounds, gardens, and outdoor recreational areas complement the interior features of the common house.

Third, the pedestrian-friendly site design (with parking clustered on the perimeter) promotes interaction with neighbors and an active walking lifestyle. The entire property is designed with universal access, allowing any homeowner or guest to access any private home, common grounds and the common house. Adaptable, one-story houses will encourage successful aging in place, so that older Oklahomans are not forced into nursing homes.

Above Oakcreek site plan
Opposite top Interior of a private house
Opposite bottom Rendering of the renovated common house

Client Goals and Design Team Solutions

1 Client Goal: Belonging to something bigger than myself.

Design team solution: Stillwater Cohousing provides the framework for these active adults to age-in-place. The residents are committed to living in a sustainable community, as well as working with each other to keep the community vibrant.

2 Client Goal: Save time, energy, and money by sharing.

Design team solution: By designing the community around the people and not the cars, residents rely on each other to help out, whether it's a group trip to the grocery store or borrowing a cup of sugar from your neighbor.

3 Client Goal: Fun.

Design team solution: The site is designed to allow for ample outdoor space, including both natural areas and constructed space, such as the common terrace. The terrace is multi-functional and can be used for common dinners, music concerts, game nights, or catching up with your neighbor.

Major Design Objectives and/or Project Challenges and the Related Responses

1 Little cottages: The cohousing community was designed for the residents to say, "I feel like I'm on vacation all of the time." The private houses are clustered into three 8-unit pods, which support the notion of being on vacation. The pods help balance the residents' private space with the common space by creating both private backyards and public front yards.

2 Preserving the existing structure: An existing building on the site was remodeled to become the common house. This not only cut down on construction costs, but also keeps a piece of history on the site.

3 Sustainable design: The houses are small, with windows and doors on each side. Natural ventilation is achievable through this, and eliminates the need for air conditioning. Every unit was designed to reduce the use of mechanical heating or cooling.

Opposite top Rendering of the front of a private house building
Opposite bottom Perspective rendering of the 8-unit private house pod

Unique Context

Oakcreek Community is a senior cohousing facility comprising like-minded people and founded on the principles of community, participatory decision-making, and problem solving that offers sustainability and affordability to its members, who are active adults of diverse talents, and to whom personal and communal growth is important. The site was originally zoned for single family living, but was rezoned to accommodate a new 24-house senior cohousing community. Residents at Oakcreek enjoy a sense of belonging to something bigger than themselves and contributing to a whole that is larger than its parts—yet maintain their own sense of autonomy.

The community is conveniently located just a mile and a half from historic Main Street in Stillwater, Oklahoma, and even closer to other amenities and services like banks, churches, movies, grocery stores, a health center, and a shopping center. Natural landmarks, like Boone Lake and the Kameoka Trail, which passes just west of the community, provide a place for recreation and exercise. This active adult community is designed to encourage naturally occurring community, as residents come and go in their daily activities.

Environmental Sustainability & Energy Conservation

In order for Oakcreek to achieve the goal of reducing its carbon footprint, the owner needed to collectively rethink how to allow seniors to achieve their full potential during their last 20 to 30 years, while simultaneously addressing environmental concerns. Oakcreek community provides the opportunity for Stillwater seniors to be part of the solution.

Extensive paths along the site, resources on-hand, common meals, geothermal heating/cooling, super-insulation, and large overhangs ("sombreros"), which save the building from the hot Oklahoma sun, are all examples of how this community reduces its carbon footprint. The Oakcreek community works together, whether that means cooking or taking care of someone who is sick.

Advanced Technology

The residents of Oakcreek decided on integrating a ground source heat pump into their project. Thanks to a federal subsidy, the community was able to make this happen. The geothermal heating and cooling system runs water through pipes that are 60 meters underground. During the hot summers, the cool air from the ground is brought into the home, which cools the space with little to no energy. This cuts down on money and space for mechanical systems and creates a comfortable living environment.

Radiant barriers were also used on the project to prevent solar heat from entering through the roof. This barrier keeps the attic and house cooler than the average home. In Oklahoma, there are 1,921 cooling degree-days (CDD), which indicates the amount of energy needed to cool a home. The radiant barriers reduce the amount of energy needed to cool, because it keeps the house cool day by day.

Design & Philosophy of Care

At Oakcreek, the residents wanted to prevent institutionalized care. Claire Dowers-Nichols, the Community Services Director for Oklahoma Department of Human Services, Aging Services Division, reports that "Oklahoma has 28,000 nursing home beds, of which 25,000 are occupied and it is estimated that 25–30 per cent of these are inappropriate placements." By creating architecture and communities where people can age-in-place, it means people can live with their family, friends, and neighbors, while staying in the comfort of their own home.

Integration of Residents with the Broader Community

Oakcreek residents have the opportunity to enjoy the cultural, educational, and sports activities that a university town has to offer. Among other things, Stillwater is home to Oklahoma State University's fine arts programs, Allied Arts, and Osher Lifelong Learning Institute—which offer an array of cultural and educational opportunities at reasonable costs.

The community is very friendly while being economically, racially, and culturally diverse with churches and worship centers for many faith traditions. Stillwater has been designated as Oklahoma's first Certified Retirement Community, meaning that Stillwater is working to provide recreational opportunities, housing, products, and services that make this a very desirable location for retirees to enjoy their retirement years. The Oakcreek community allows residents to enjoy a high-functioning community where people relate and stay connected naturally.

But most importantly, this community gives residents the "safe harbor" necessary for them to have the support and confidence to go out to elder the rest of the community.

Opposite top Residents gathering on the common terrace
Opposite bottom Residents enjoying a small lunch on the common terrace

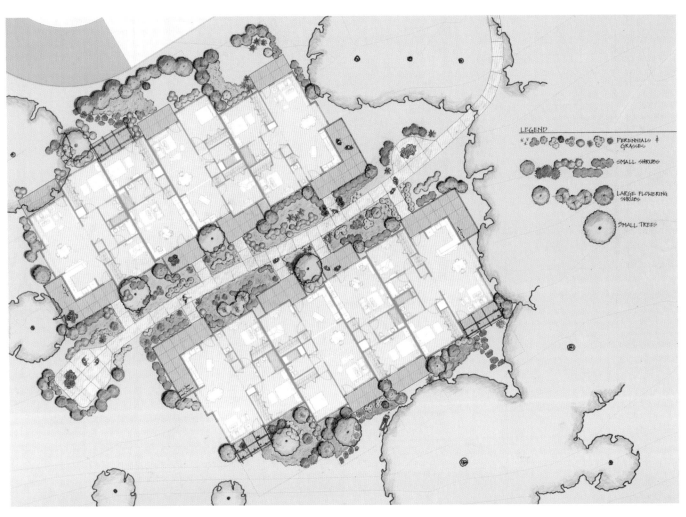

Staffing

Total number of staff at this facility None, but the facility is designed to welcome a caregiver at a later date

Number of management staff Stillwater Cohousing is completely self-managed

Number of care staff (registered nursing and direct care staff) None, but the facility is designed to welcome a caregiver at a later date

Direct care hours per day per client Currently none, except for neighbors

Number of other staff (e.g. maintenance, housekeeping, food services) Currently none, except for neighbors

Project Capacity and Numbers of Units

Independent living cottages/villas 24

Breakdown of Independent Living Units

One bedroom units 6
Typical size per unit 65m²

Two bedroom units 18
Typical size per unit 102m²

Resident/Client Age

Current average age 60–85 years old

Resident/Client Fees and Funding

Entry fee or unit purchase Yes ($150,000 to $350,000)

Client Monthly Funding Private (out-of-pocket) pay

As independent care, residents range from 60 to 85 years. They are and have been very active members of the larger community. Many of them have been caregivers, and seek a caring, giving, co-operative environment for caregivers.

There are no staff at Stillwater Senior Cohousing. The community is self-managed, where the residents rely on each other and neighbors for any other support. However, the cohousing was designed to accommodate caregivers at any given time.

Opposite top The 8-unit pod landscape plan by Karin Kaufman of Karin Kaufman Landscape Architect

Opposite bottom An impromptu music concert on the common terrace

Below A resident watering flowers in front of her private house

Taube Koret Campus for Jewish Life

Palo Alto, California, USA
Alan Sataloff / Steinberg Architects

Project type Active Senior/
Independent Living Residence,
Assisted Living/Hostel Residence,
Community-Based Services/
Multi-Level Care/Continuing Care
Retirement Communities, Special
Care Residence (for those with
dementia), Skilled Nursing Care
Residence

Site location Urban

Site size 3.4 hectares

Building area 40,160m²

Total building cost US$178 million

Date completed September 2009

Photography Tim Griffith

Owner's Statement

The Taube Koret Campus for Jewish Life is a welcoming, innovative, intergenerational destination where individuals and families can live, learn, play and connect. Anchored by a world-class community center—Oshman Family Jewish Community Center—and a modern senior living community—Moldaw Family Residences—the campus is designed to engage the region's diverse Jewish community and help reenergize the South Palo Alto area. Through its diverse programmatic mix, the new campus invites the broader community to participate in extensive educational, social, cultural, and recreational opportunities offered in a Jewish context, including enhanced programs and services in early childhood education, after-school care, day camps and enrichment programs for children, family activities, and an extensive offering of activities for adults and teens.

Below Cityscape
Opposite top Town square, the most public of the outdoor rooms
Opposite bottom Midrahov (walkstreet), with housing above public facilities

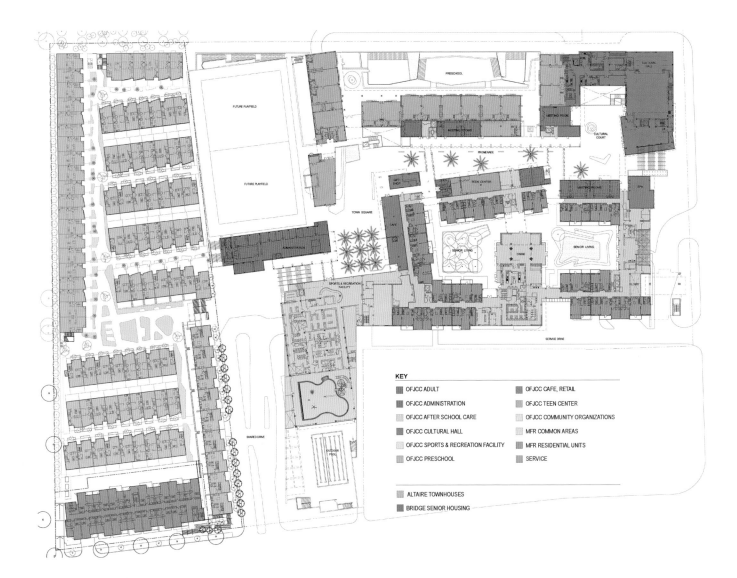

KEY

	OFJCC ADULT		OFJCC CAFE, RETAIL
	OFJCC ADMINISTRATION		OFJCC TEEN CENTER
	OFJCC AFTER SCHOOL CARE		OFJCC COMMUNITY ORGANIZATIONS
	OFJCC CULTURAL HALL		MFR COMMON AREAS
	OFJCC SPORTS & RECREATION FACILITY		MFR RESIDENTIAL UNITS
	OFJCC PRESCHOOL		SERVICE

	ALTAIRE TOWNHOUSES
	BRIDGE SENIOR HOUSING

Architect's Statement

The Taube Koret Campus for Jewish Life is a new paradigm in senior housing—an intergenerational community that combines time-proven traditional urban planning principles, based on the structure of a medieval city, with contemporary architecture appropriate to Silicon Valley. The campus is an urban village—a residential model that provides ample opportunities that enable seniors to stay close to home or participate in activities with the larger Palo Alto community. Meandering, asymmetric "walk streets" create a safe environment and encourage social connections, both spontaneous and planned.

Top Intergenerational campus master plan
Right Contemplative senior garden
Opposite top Cultural court
Opposite bottom Senior courtyard designed to accommodate intergenerational activities

172

Client Goals and Design Team Solutions

1 Client Goal: An intergenerational community. The campus is founded on the belief that everyone—from children to adults to seniors—benefits from the opportunity to interact with a diverse group of people of all ages on a daily basis. The Taube Koret Center for Jewish Life is designed to maximize opportunities for both casual and planned interactions, from organized activities to family events to casual strolls through the town square. Each of the eight houses is a unique community, oriented toward one of the outdoor rooms, offering seniors the option to live in a very active space with a strong focus on youth, fitness, or cultural activities. Other rooms overlook internal program spaces, which have less interaction with people from outside the senior living community.

2 Client Goal: Maintaining seniors' independence. The community is designed to offer a wide range of options for seniors to maintain their independence and to achieve a balance between maintaining their privacy and staying connected to the larger community. By combining senior living with a large community center, residents have direct access to a 4,645-square meter facility with a broad range of activities. In addition, smaller activity centers are located both horizontally and vertically within each neighborhood. So they have the choice of using health and wellness facilities within their own neighborhood or using one of the shared activity centers, which enable them to get to know residents of other neighborhoods.

3 Client Goal: Creating a third generation of senior housing. The Taube Koret Campus for Jewish Life represents the third generation of senior housing. While the first generation sequestered its residents from the surrounding community and the second generation emphasized lifelong learning opportunities, the Taube Koret Campus for Jewish Life is an urban village—a residential model that provides ample opportunities for engagement with the outside environment. The community has all the vitality of a city, without the challenges that make urban living difficult for seniors, such as level changes or traffic. It includes a broad range of residential unit types, depending on the seniors' ability to continue living independently. Some suites provide living space for live-in home health care workers, who can provide 24-hour support while enabling senior residents to maintain their privacy.

Major Design Objectives and/or Project Challenges and the Related Responses

1 Growth beyond the original plan: As the program developed, the senior housing component grew from a planned 7,430-square meter, stand-alone assisted living facility into a 22,300-square meter continuum of care retirement community. The architects embraced this challenge by seamlessly integrating facilities both horizontally and vertically in order to create a village-like scale. The vertical stacking also helped define a series of outdoor rooms that encourage socialization. These outdoor rooms include the Town Square, the Midrachov (walk street), a cultural courtyard, a children's courtyard, and senior housing courtyards uniquely designed to accommodate the visual and movement sensitivities of the elderly.

2 Building on a 4-meter elevation: Because the Taube Koret Campus for Jewish Life was built on a brownfield site, the entire community had to be elevated on a 4-meter platform. The architects were able to use this feature to their advantage by locating all parking at grade and creating a plaza at an elevation of over 4 meters. The plaza is a car-free community with modern architecture superimposed over a plan with the characteristics of a medieval city. The result is a series of meandering, asymmetric walk streets where one moves from one outdoor room, underneath bridges or through portals, to another outdoor room experience.

3 Creating distinct areas of activity: When the two entities—Jewish Home and Jewish Community Center—began their partnership, their first instinct was to create distinct, segregated areas of activity—a residential area, and a community center. The architects worked with both partners to demonstrate the benefits of interconnecting horizontally and vertically through the sharing of cultural, food, service, and maintenance facilities. By teaming together, shared opportunities were created that neither partner could have created on their own. This relationship created broad benefits for the senior housing residents, JCC members, and the Palo Alto community.

Opposite Utilizing organic materials

Unique Context

In order to take advantage of Northern California's moderate climate and encourage seniors to remain active and independent, a series of outdoor rooms make up the heart of the community. The town square is a hub for residents and visitors, offering easy access to restaurants, fitness facilities, preschool, administrative offices, and afterschool activities. The cultural courtyard hosts indoor/ outdoor social/cultural events for campus and off-campus users. The children's courtyard houses preschool and afterschool activities. Senior housing courtyards are uniquely designed to accommodate the visual and movement challenges of the elderly.

The campus was designed to have broad appeal to the Bay Area Jewish community, enabling residents to live in a community with other Jewish seniors without sequestering them from society. The social, cultural, and fitness activities offered by the Jewish Community Center (JCC) have a Jewish cultural focus, but also appeal to the large percentage of JCC members who are non-Jews; approximately 40 per cent of the JCC's membership is non-Jewish. In addition, the Taube Koret Campus for Jewish Life partners with local arts and cultural organizations to create further opportunities to share resources. For example, the Palo Alto Chamber Orchestra uses the cultural hall three times a year for free. In return, they play a free concert once a month in one of the outdoor squares.

Environmental Sustainability & Energy Conservation

The campus has a highly efficient energy system that results in an overall efficiency of 28 per cent above building code requirements; more than 90 per cent of the rooms have a view of the outdoors and over 75 per cent of these rooms receive enough natural light during daylight hours, so not much artificial light is needed; and an integrated building management system based on occupancy sensors controls the lighting, heating, and air conditioning systems. Portable water usage is reduced by approximately 32 per cent by the use of low-flow sinks and showers and low-flush or dual-flush toilets. Water usage for landscaping is reduced by approximately 52 per cent by planting only drought-resistant and native plants, using drip irrigation to reduce evaporation, and use of moisture-retaining mulch. The campus also features an onsite recycling program.

Advanced Technology

The campus is designed to incorporate state-of-the-art systems and equipment wherever possible, and this technology is found in the lighting, security, telephone, mechanical, and heating and cooling systems. A few examples include: a single card key for each resident, which allows entrance into residence buildings, their individual unit, and various other campus facilities; occupancy sensors that turn on lighting, heating, and air conditioning systems when rooms are occupied and turns them off when empty; and aerobic equipment in the sports and wellness complex are hooked up to a central computer that uploads new workout routines, monitors repairs, and even sends updates to users while exercising.

Design and Philosophy of Care

The senior living residences applied the small-house concepts of scale, outside access, and staffing to residential/independent living; eight small-scale residences are built and connected to each other. Each provides both small group living and ready access to the outdoors, natural light, short-cuts, and each has a distinctive name and social amenities. The goal was to reduce the scale and increase motivation to engage, including in the intergenerational programs. Households are also designed for Memory Care Assisted Living (11 with full programs, country kitchens and dining), and two households for those entering Assisted Living (12 with distinctive country kitchens, dining and programs, as well as full use of campus programs).

Integration of Residents with the Broader Community

The Jewish Community Center includes a gymnasium, three swimming pools, and 12,000 square meters of fitness, yoga, and classes that draw thousands from all over the greater Palo Alto. Membership is included in one's residency and it sits directly adjacent to the seniors' residences. The T'enna Preschool and Leslie Family Early Childhood and Family Education Center sit directly under several floors of the residential living and seniors maintain the children's garden/play area (visible from the residences above). The Schultz Cultural Arts Hall is a spectacular center for year-round performances, lectures, and cultural events, and it is both connected and in view of the residences.

Opposite top View of the Midrahov (walkstreet) from one of the senior activity spaces
Opposite bottom Memory window at entry to Memory Support unit

Project Capacity and Numbers of Units

Independent living apartments 170

Assisted living/hostel care 12

Special care for persons with dementia 11

Fitness/rehab/wellness/pool(s) and related areas
(daily visits) 600–1,000

Early childhood education 100

Social community 500–2,000

Breakdown of Independent Living Units

One bedroom units 74
Typical size per unit 79m²

Two bedroom units 84
Typical size per unit 93m²

Two bedroom plus units 12
Typical size per unit 140m²

Breakdown of Assisted Living/Hostel Care Units

One bedroom units 12
Typical size per unit 60m²

Breakdown of Dementia Special Care Units

Studio/bed-sit units 11
Typical size per unit 29m²

Resident/Client Age

Current average age 83 years old
Average age upon entry 80 years old

Opposite top Senior dining room
Opposite bottom Cultural hall with retractable theater seating
Below Intergenerational hot water pool with zero depth access

Union Life Shenyang Retirement Community

Union Life / Shenyang, China, Liaoning Provence
LRS Architects

Project type Multi-Level Care/
Continuing Care Retirement
Communities

Site location Suburban

Site size 50,572m²

Building footprint 13,863m²

Building area 60,893m²

Total building cost US$53,671,700

Building cost US$885m²

Date completed To be confirmed

Owner's Statement

Responding to emerging social and cultural needs, a comprehensive master plan
is underway in Shenyang, China, that will address the specific needs for the aging
population. The owner's vision begins with a successful design and planning approach
that accommodates seniors who want more options in senior facilities.

This project will be the largest, most comprehensive, modern, and culturally significant
senior community in Northeast China. The senior community component is part of a
three-phase master plan. Other phases will provide residential and community services
for an independent resident population.

This campus will accommodate residents who need assisted, skilled, and memory care
services. Lifestyle services include medical rehabilitation, nursing, health, leisure, and
life-long learning, all woven into the local Chinese culture. One unique component to the
overall vision is directly adjacent to the campus: a purpose-designed commercial and
active senior lifestyle center that will support this project and other community outreach
functions and needs.

Project challenges were mainly site-driven, due to shape, slope, and the northern building
code requirements. Once resolved, the design team achieved the targeted building
program and efficiency ratio that the owner demanded. The collaborative effort by all the
stakeholders throughout the design process is reflected in the creative solutions.

Above Assisted Living entry elevation
Opposite top Assisted Living entry
Opposite bottom Master plan aerial view

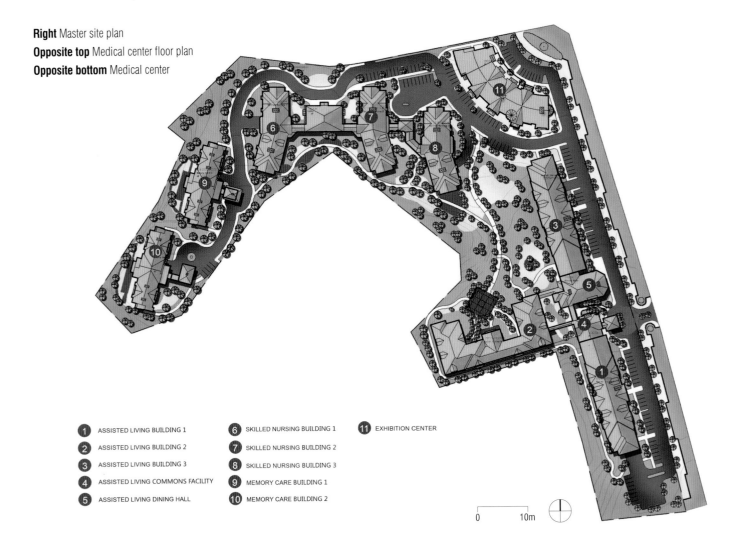

Right Master site plan
Opposite top Medical center floor plan
Opposite bottom Medical center

1 ASSISTED LIVING BUILDING 1
2 ASSISTED LIVING BUILDING 2
3 ASSISTED LIVING BUILDING 3
4 ASSISTED LIVING COMMONS FACILITY
5 ASSISTED LIVING DINING HALL

6 SKILLED NURSING BUILDING 1
7 SKILLED NURSING BUILDING 2
8 SKILLED NURSING BUILDING 3
9 MEMORY CARE BUILDING 1
10 MEMORY CARE BUILDING 2

11 EXHIBITION CENTER

0   10m

Architect's Statement

This Retirement Community offers three levels of residential living care: Assisted Living, Skilled Nursing, and Memory Care. The fourth component is the Exhibition/ Medical Services Building that will offer services to this campus, as well as the outside community.

Architectural design criteria integrated into the Union Life Vision include:

- Signature campus, offering residents a sense of community and home;

- Retirement community, accommodating residents' changing levels of care and needs;

- Each area (Assisted Living, Skilled Nursing, and Memory Care) has clearly organized common area plans, which allow easy campus navigation;

- Keeping services and support safe and separated from resident access, both internal and external;

- Developing a campus that engages residents in wellness and life-long learning activities;

- Incorporating Union Life's design aesthetic based on traditional "English Manor" style architecture, integrating references to late-medieval country houses;

- Design cues from the exterior architecture are integrated into interior design elements;

- Creating a framework of sustainable practices for long-term energy savings and reduced environmental impact.

Design challenges from site shape, slope, and solar/ shadow requirements affected every decision for building placement. Client goals for building function and operational efficiency were carefully integrated.

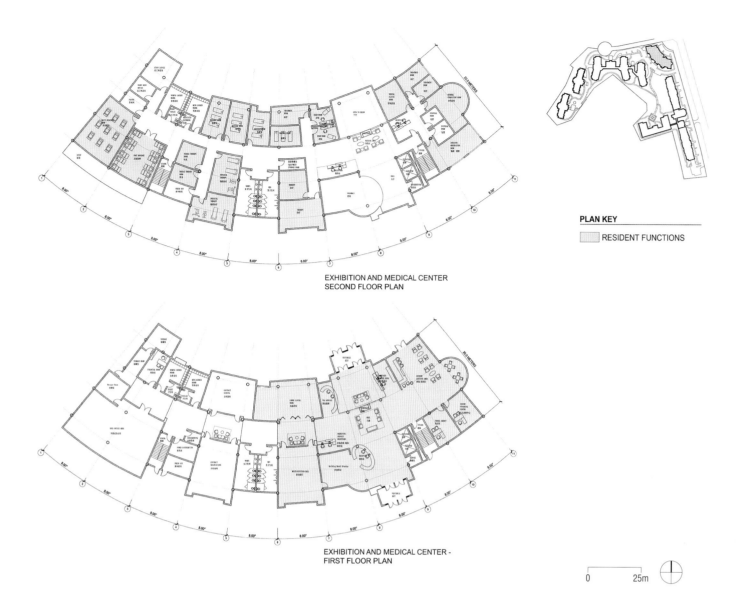

EXHIBITION AND MEDICAL CENTER
SECOND FLOOR PLAN

EXHIBITION AND MEDICAL CENTER -
FIRST FLOOR PLAN

PLAN KEY

RESIDENT FUNCTIONS

0   25m

Union Life Shenyang Retirement Community   183

Client Goals and Design Team Solutions

1 **Client goal:** This project will be a landmark senior living community. Union Life intends to be a leading provider for high-level care and services for seniors.

Design team solution: Union Life will provide full-service amenities from active living to holistic health care services that this region in China has not experienced before. The results will be impressive and ambitious. Included in the design program is a separate medical building that will provide both Chinese and Western medicine services, including herbal and injection-type therapy. These services are convenient for all residents and the nearby independent residents of the community.

2 **Client goal:** The design intent direction from Union Life demanded that this be a signature project on all accounts. The architecture needs to achieve a sense of permanence and quality, for both exterior and interior design. The selection of materials needs to withstand the northern climate and complement the architecture and detail.

Design team solution: English Style architecture and design influences were mandated as the genesis for all aspects of the Shenyang projects. This included the use of brick, painted trim, cut stone, and steeply sloped roofs. The design solutions give a "timeless" sense of place that will endure with the culture and senior lifestyle.

3 **Client goal:** A functional and efficient collaborative planning approach, with building performance and utilization as key factors, focused on floor plate layout that affects the overall building area and costs. The goal was to maximize personal and private space, while controlling common and support space areas.

Design team solution: Working with a challenging site and slope, the results achieved were 62 per cent building efficiency averaged for all the residential care program areas: Assisted Living, Skilled Nursing, and Memory Care. The assisted living buildings alone achieved 69.9 per cent efficiency; the goal set by Union Life is 70 per cent. Common area circulation space is the result of building clusters arranged on this challenged site.

Major Design Objectives and/or Project Challenges and the Related Responses

1 **Sun exposure, shadows, site slope and elevation:** The greatest challenge from a master plan approach is the local building/planning code mandate that every living unit must have at least two hours' direct sun exposure on December 22, the winter solstice. The second challenge was that one building cannot cast shadows onto another building, preventing the required two hours of sun on December 22. The third factor, further complicating the first two issues, is site slope and elevation change between buildings. The team produced a campus plan with all but one building oriented north–south to maximize the solar exposure and be carefully positioned so as not to cast shadows on adjacent buildings.

2 **Crafting a lifestyle of culture:** A primary Union Life design directive was crafting a "lifestyle of culture" that shifts away from the institutional feel prevalent in China senior housing. The design team focused on achieving the feeling of hospitality for all levels of care and components of the campus. This approach assures choices for dining, activities, and services within richly designed spaces offering formal to informal gatherings and lounge options, including tearooms, game rooms for mahjong, tai chi areas, and shi (poetry) reading rooms. This culture-based lifestyle offers residents the dignity, privacy, and independence to grow and be nurtured in a hospitality-based community.

3 **Catering to a large number of residents:** Providing meals for a resident population in excess of a thousand—1,027 in this case—is not uncommon in China. The design team's challenge was to educate the client about the need for more than one central kitchen to serve three residential care areas (Assisted Living, Skilled Nursing, and Memory Care). Three separate building clusters were created, each with their own unique operations and service access. Most importantly, the buildings are not connected and do not have a grand central kitchen. The solution was to provide two main kitchens. One serves Assisted Living alone and the other, within the Skilled Nursing building, provides prepared food, delivered to the Memory Care building.

Opposite top Memory Care dining and activity areas
Opposite bottom Memory Care plans

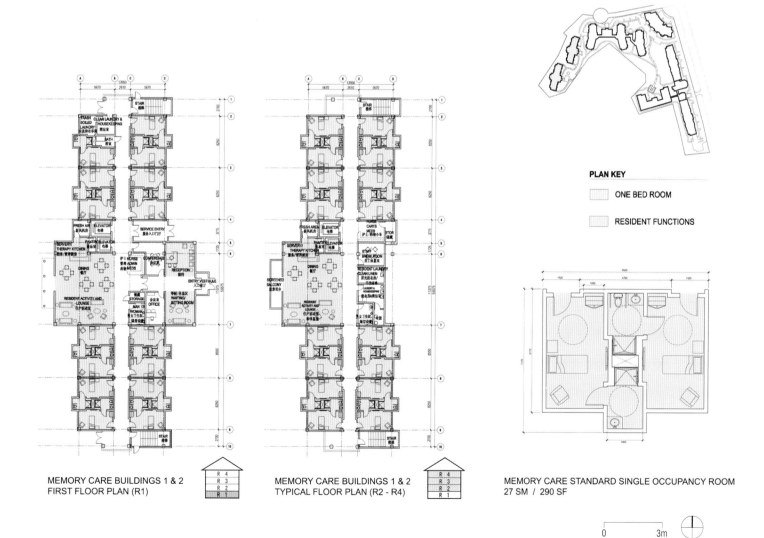

PLAN KEY

ONE BED ROOM

RESIDENT FUNCTIONS

MEMORY CARE BUILDINGS 1 & 2
FIRST FLOOR PLAN (R1)

MEMORY CARE BUILDINGS 1 & 2
TYPICAL FLOOR PLAN (R2 - R4)

MEMORY CARE STANDARD SINGLE OCCUPANCY ROOM
27 SM / 290 SF

0   3m

Above Assisted Living dining
Below Assisted Living plans
Opposite Assisted Living unit plans

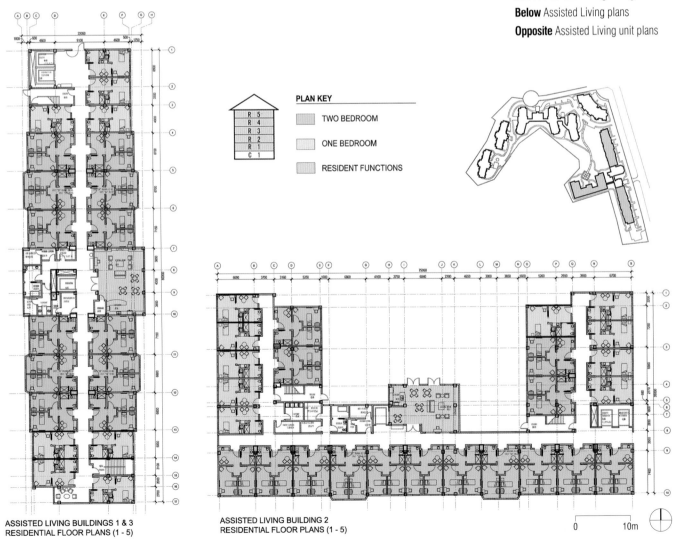

PLAN KEY

	TWO BEDROOM
	ONE BEDROOM
	RESIDENT FUNCTIONS

ASSISTED LIVING BUILDINGS 1 & 3
RESIDENTIAL FLOOR PLANS (1 - 5)

ASSISTED LIVING BUILDING 2
RESIDENTIAL FLOOR PLANS (1 - 5)

0   10m

Unique Context

One compelling feature for this project is the greater master plan designed for this 330-acre undeveloped area in Shenyang, also called the "Green Lung" because of the natural scenic beauty of the mountains and rivers. This project will have, to its benefit, resources of a new community and resident population that will promote exchange of services, culture, and a healthy livable environment. Within the greater master plan, new business and research talent will move into the region, creating families for generations.

In parallel with this campus is the design of the Shenyang commercial site, directly across the road, and within walking distance. This site will support the senior residents and the greater community with five main areas of service; Arts and Entertainment, Daily Dining, Sports and Fitness, Leisure and Gathering, and Union College.

Connected to this by footbridges across a small river are a new temple, meditation hall, and lodge for monks. All of these activities, services, and facilities are arranged around an elliptical master plan that has a "grand central park." This new town center will provide opportunity on those warm summer evenings to dance in the park or fly a kite, as everyone enjoys in China.

Environmental Sustainability & Energy Conservation

The beautiful features for this rugged mountainous region are the natural rocks, distant mountains, and local rivers. The site design will address the slope and grading issues, providing senior-sensitive pathways interconnecting buildings, plazas, and gardens.

Extreme cool winters and warm summers are demanding on energy resources. The goal is to provide water-saving fixtures, native drought-tolerant plant material and energy-saving equipment and lighting. Resident on-site gardening and composting will provide vegetable production used in the campus kitchens. Wind and sun energy can be harvested with the use of hybrid solar- and wind-driven site lighting for roadways and pedestrian walks.

Advanced Technology

Proposed is the adoption of a "paperless" resident data, records, and wellness monitor system. The technology available will aid staff and management, saving time and resources by using electronic and wireless products. All systems control and monitor residents' safety and wellness, environmental conditions, and allow communication with residents. These systems will give management reports about individual resident needs, as well as staff performance, providing management the opportunity to adjust strategies as necessary. Advanced building technology will include maximum thermal insulation protection in the exterior walls and roofs for energy saving in extremely low temperatures in winter, as well as the high summer heat.

Design & Philosophy of Care

The new philosophy of care introduced at Shenyang revolutionizes thinking about Chinese seniors, their lives and futures. The program will allow seniors to be introduced to a new healthy, active, and enriched life-long learning environment. In past generations, seniors focused on their families rather than themselves.

China's seniors mostly come from dense urban areas and normally only dream of living their retirement years in a natural, healthy, and supportive community with fellow residents. Union Life at Shenyang is the gateway offering complete integrated services: a resident living area with three levels (Assisted Living, Skilled Nursing, Memory Care), health and medical center, 5-star hospitality, fitness center, and rehabilitation.

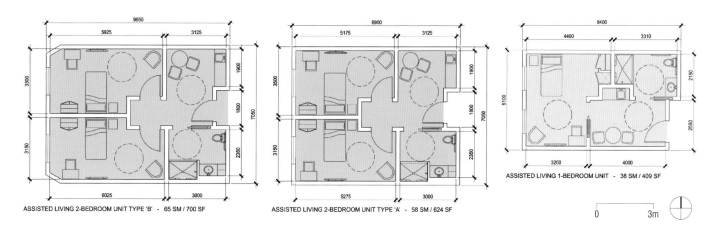

ASSISTED LIVING 2-BEDROOM UNIT TYPE 'B' - 65 SM / 700 SF

ASSISTED LIVING 2-BEDROOM UNIT TYPE 'A' - 58 SM / 624 SF

ASSISTED LIVING 1-BEDROOM UNIT - 38 SM / 409 SF

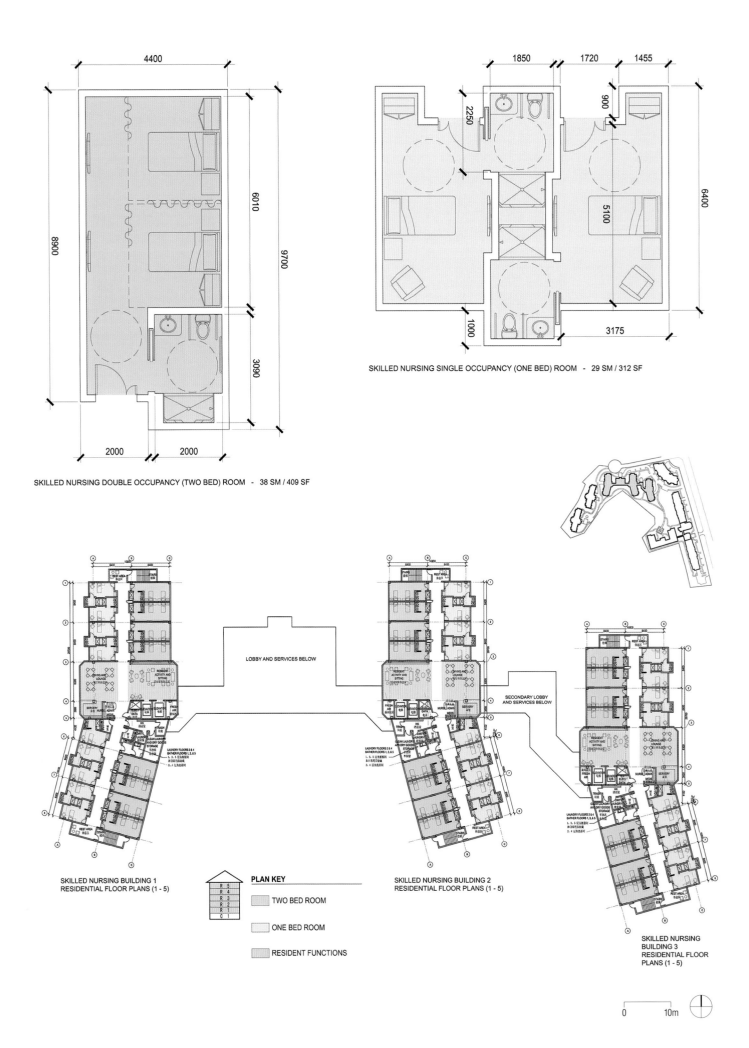

4400

8900

6010

9700

3090

2000   **2000**

SKILLED NURSING DOUBLE OCCUPANCY (TWO BED) ROOM - 38 SM / 409 SF

1850   **1720**   **1455**

2250

900

5100

6400

1000

3175

SKILLED NURSING SINGLE OCCUPANCY (ONE BED) ROOM - 29 SM / 312 SF

LOBBY AND SERVICES BELOW

SECONDARY LOBBY
AND SERVICES BELOW

SKILLED NURSING BUILDING 1
RESIDENTIAL FLOOR PLANS (1 - 5)

PLAN KEY

TWO BED ROOM

ONE BED ROOM

RESIDENT FUNCTIONS

SKILLED NURSING BUILDING 2
RESIDENTIAL FLOOR PLANS (1 - 5)

SKILLED NURSING
BUILDING 3
RESIDENTIAL FLOOR
PLANS (1 - 5)

0   10m

Project Capacity and Numbers of Units

Assisted living/hostel care (units) 329

Special care for persons with dementia 126

Skilled nursing care (beds) 263

Kitchen (daily meals served) 3,081, plus staff

Breakdown of Assisted Living/Hostel Care Units

One bedroom units 132
Typical size per unit 38m²

Two bedroom units 197
Typical size per unit 61.5m²

Breakdown of Dementia Special Care Units

One bedroom units 126
Typical size per unit 27m²

Breakdown of Skilled Nursing Care Units

One bed/single occupancy rooms 139
Typical size per unit 29m²

Two bed/double occupancy rooms 124
Typical size per unit 38m²

Resident/Client Age

Current average age 65 years old
Age upon entry 60 years old

Resident/Client Fees and Funding

Entry fee yes
Client Monthly Funding Private (out-of-pocket) pay

Opposite top Skilled Nursing unit plans
Opposite bottom Skilled Nursing buildings
Below left Skilled Nursing rehabilitation
Below right Skilled Nursing dining
Bottom Skilled Nursing activity area

Valley View Senior Housing

American Canyon, California, USA

**Satellite Affordable Housing Association (SAHA) /
McCamant & Durrett Architects**

Project type Active Senior/
Independent Living Residence,
Community-Based Services,
Subsidized Affordable
Independent Living

Site location Suburban

Site size 1.5 hectares

Building footprint 3,135m²

Building area 3,500m²

Total building cost Projected
US$7.5 million

Building cost Projected US$2,153/m²

Date completed Scheduled for 2015

Photography Charles Durrett

Owner's Statement

Valley View is an affordable, rental senior housing development on a 1.5-hectare site with 70 dwelling units, a clubhouse, open space and parking. The site is sloped, creating a hillside town with meandering paths, electric vehicle charging stations, garden beds, bocce ball court, and a common terrace.

Development for the site began in 2005 when a 35-unit single-family project was approved. However, the project stalled in 2008, and fell into foreclosure. Valley View Senior Housing began with a Request for Proposal (RFP) from the City of American Canyon in California. The RFP was approved by the City Council in 2011, and the Satellite Affordable Housing Association was chosen in 2012, out of 30 designs, to move forward with a design proposal for the site.

The City designated the site as an affordable senior rental housing project funded in part by the City of American Canyon, and is zoned medium density residential. The City's goal is to create a high-quality project that complies with the city's multifamily design standards to enhance the neighborhood and set the character for future projects in the medium-density residential zoning district. This project will provide the all-important opportunity for residents, many long-term, to remain in the community that they have loved, and that loves them.

Right Rendered elevation of the clubhouse entrance off the main road

Opposite Perspective of the meandering walkway that leads to residences

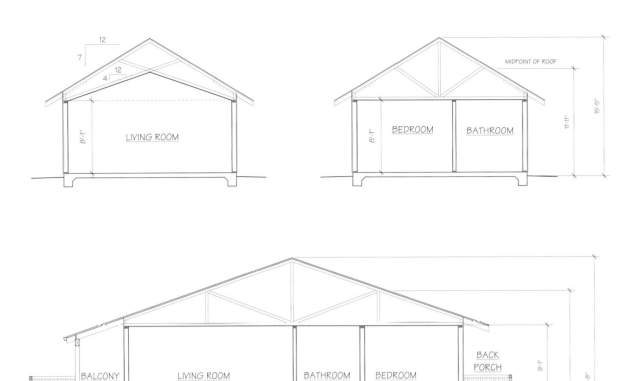

Top Cottage sections

Architect's Statement

Satellite Affordable Housing Association (SAHA), which is the developer and manager of the project, proposes to create approximately 70 cottage-style units on the site, all of which will be affordable to very low and extremely low-income seniors aged 55 and over. The senior community will offer a high level of amenities as well as on-site services for older adults with modest financial means. Residents will enjoy a beautifully landscaped site that incorporates the highest standards of green building and sustainable design, as well as a robust selection of on-site services and activities to support wellness, independent living, and aging-in-place.

The housing development is envisioned to be a vibrant community that complements the character of the existing single-family neighborhood while achieving a density that promotes financial feasibility and long-term operational sustainability. The approach to the project and site is to incorporate as much of the existing grading and retaining walls as possible. This avoids unnecessary waste of materials and labor, with the added potential for overall cost savings. The result is a walkable hillside development of charming cottages, peripheral parking, meandering paths, active recreation, a community garden, and a community clubhouse, all working to create a sense of place that is unique to American Canyon, California.

Top Cottage sections
Above Two-story stacked flats section
Opposite top Two-unit cottage plan
Opposite middle Three-unit cottage plan
Opposite bottom Two-story stacked flats second floor plan

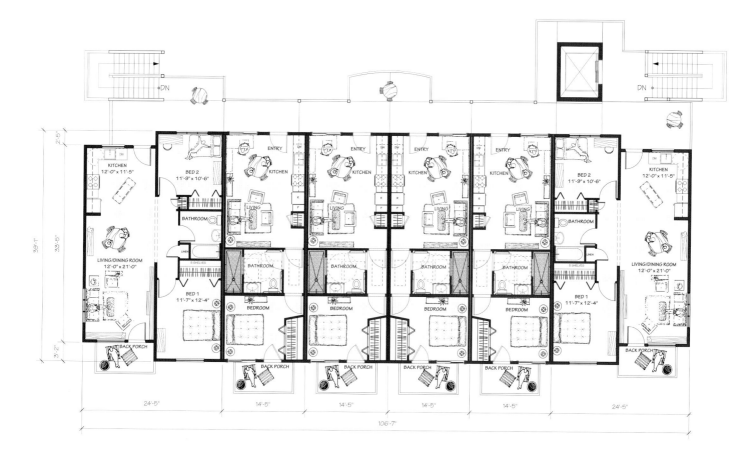

Below Typical clubhouse section
Bottom Clubhouse floor plan
Opposite top Clubhouse section at Great Room roof light
Opposite bottom Clubhouse section at Great Room

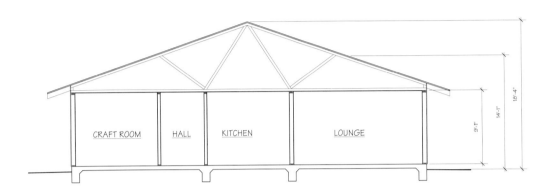

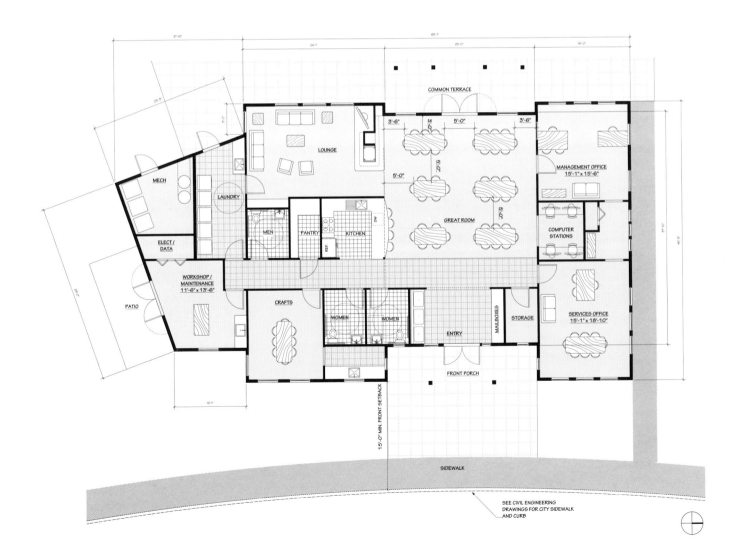

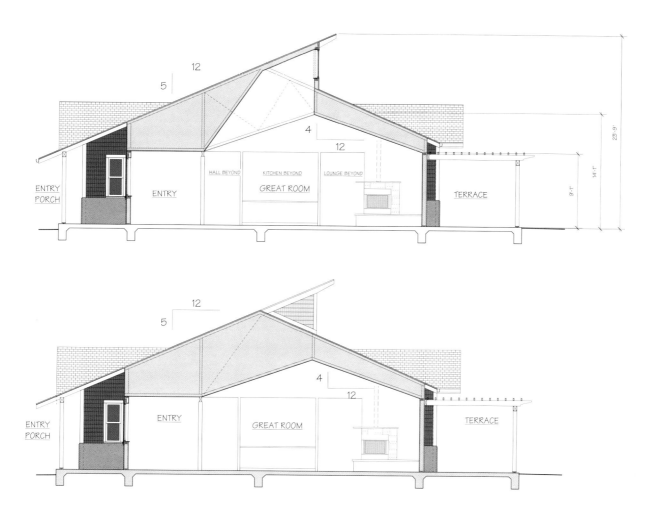

Client Goals and Design Team Solutions

1 Client Goal: Developing an affordable senior rental project.

Design team solution: SAHA, an experienced affordable housing developer, will create affordable rental units to provide very low to extremely low income seniors with a place to live.

2 Client Goal: Including amenities in the project.

Design team solution: Senior communities typically have a community room where games, meals, and other services are offered. However, the spaces are purposeful, yet rarely used. The residents at Valley View will be encouraged through site design to engage with each other, whether it's bocce ball, cards, gardening, or helping fold laundry. Outdoor terraces, balconies, courtyards, and gazebos support these activities.

3 Client Goal: Providing excellent rental management experience.

Design team solution: All SAHA projects have an on-site manager who will live on the property. Different from senior cohousing communities, the manager is there to take care of the property, since the residents rent and do not own their homes.

Major Design Objectives and/or Project Challenges and the Related Responses

1 Hill-town: Valley View is designed to take on characteristics of hill-towns you might see in Europe, except that it will be designed to be wheelchair accessible. It is uncommon to see a senior community on a hillside, but this project has various options for getting around the site, whether it s walking on the meandering paths or by using an electric cart.

2 Retain concrete walls that exist onsite: The previous development, accepted by the City before foreclosure, got as far as site work. This included grading and construction of retaining walls. The walls remain in the new design and help form the clustered cottages on the site.

3 Providing needed frontage improvements: Theresa Avenue, where the site is located, has few street trees. The project will integrate improvements for the roadway, curbs, gutters, sidewalk, parkway landscaping, storm water, and potable water mains. The clubhouse is sited along the major frontage to help define the street edge.

Unique Context

Valley View Senior Housing's unique design creates a small hill town village within its 1.5-hectare site. The design is compact, yet integrates lots of paths and gathering nodes to encourage social interaction. This not only gets the senior residents moving, but also allows them to live an independent and active life. When you encourage social interaction through design, it gets people to connect with others and that generates community.

The parking areas are pushed towards the periphery, with the exception of one parking court that is near the clubhouse. With a different paving pattern in the court, it functions as both a parking area and an outdoor activity venue.

Valley View residents are encouraged to share resources. Drawing from a common pool, members of the community will use less and have access to more, such as extensive common facilities, community gardens, an interpretive trail, and a bike trail. They will also arrange rides and share transportation with each other to go grocery shopping, see a movie, or eat out at a restaurant. American Canyon also offers the VINE Transit, which is a bus system that loops around the entire town.

Below Elevation and section of interior street running west to east

WOOD FENCE OVER EXISTING
CONCRETE RETAINING WALL, TYP.
SEE A6.2 FOR DETAIL.

Environmental Sustainability & Energy Conservation

Valley View will be a compact development that uses multiple strategies to be an environmentally sustainable and energy conservative project. With a passive cooling and heating mentality, the units were designed to have windows on both sides for ventilation, double-pane windows and shading to slow heat from entering the houses, thick gypsum board and concrete slabs for thermal mass to take advantage of diurnal temperature variations, cool roofs to reflect and emit the sun's heat

back to the sky, and large porches to provide ample shading and provide pleasant outdoor space to take advantage of the moderate climate.

The project will also use permeable surfaces where possible to help replenish groundwater and aid in controlling erosion and pollution by permitting infiltration of runoff into underlying soil. The landscape design also aids in water conservation by using native and drought-tolerant plantings.

10'-0" MIN.

2   **ELEVATION @ COTTAGE CLUSTER A**
Scale: 3/16" = 1'-0"

1   **SITE ELEVATION @ VALLEY VIEW DRIVE**
Scale: 1" = 20 ft

Advanced Technology

Valley View homes will be the second project, through SAHA, to use a graywater irrigation system. This system takes wastewater from washing machines located in the clubhouse and will use it for landscape irrigation on the property. Given the water constraints that California and the wider world are facing, the project will work closely with the City to make the system efficient and affordable.

Solar photovoltaic panels will also be used at Valley View to reduce operating costs and shift energy use to renewable sources. Not only will these photovoltaic panels be installed on the roof, but every window facing south will have a photovoltaic awning, designed from the only contractor in the USA currently marketing this product. This will not only shade the windows from the intense sun, but will provide energy to run a ceiling fan, for example.

Design & Philosophy of Care

Valley View does not accommodate staff for caregiving. The residents instead are encouraged to stay active by utilizing the amenities and services provided both onsite and within the local community. Although not a cohousing community, Valley View is still designed for residents to work with each other and encourage interaction. The community will build friendships—people they can trust and count on.

Integration of Residents with the Broader Community

The site for Valley View Senior Housing is located 35 miles northeast of San Francisco, in southern Napa County. Although not a cohousing community, the project still incorporates a clubhouse, welcoming residents and visitors to the community. The one-story structure includes a large dining room with adjacent full kitchen facilities, a lounge area, craft room, computer lab, and laundry room. These facilities are meant for the residents, but are open to the public upon invitation.

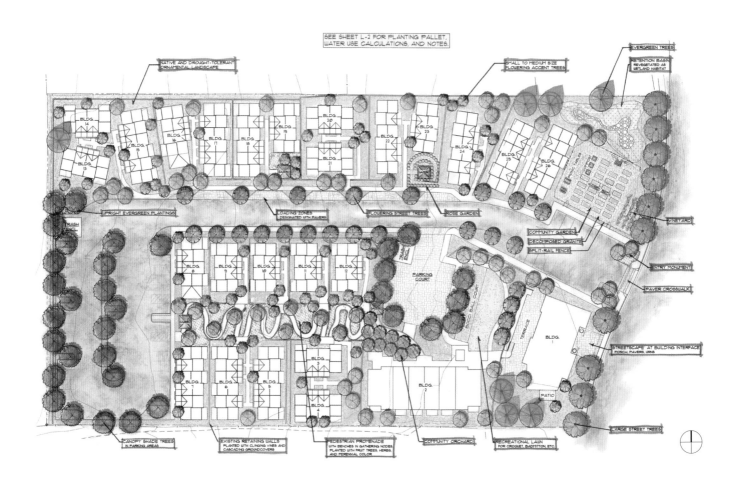

Staffing

Total number of staff at the facility One on-site manager

Number of management staff One

Number of care staff (registered nursing and direct care staff) None, but the facility is designed to welcome a caregiver at a later date

Direct care hours per day per client Currently none, except for neighbors

Number of other staff (e.g. maintenance, housekeeping, food services) One, plus site manager who does maintenance

Project Capacity and Numbers of Units

Independent living apartments 12

Independent living cottages/villas 58

Assisted living/hostel care As required

Special care for persons with dementia As required

Skilled nursing care (beds) As required

Kitchen (daily meals served) As required

Elder day care (clients) As required

Elder outreach (clients) As required

Breakdown of Independent Living Units

One bedroom units 62
Typical size per unit 49m²

Two bedroom units 8
Typical size per unit 83m²

Resident/Client Age

Average age upon entry Between 55 and 90 years

Resident/Client Fees and Funding

Entry fee or unit purchase Yes (rental price between US$430 and US$875 per month)

Client Monthly Funding Private (out-of-pocket pay), Public/government subsidies (means tested based on assets and/or income)

Valley View Senior Housing is for low to extremely low-income seniors. There are no caregivers on-site, but a caregiver can be accommodated at any point in time. There is an on-site manager who lives on-site and watches over the property, along with providing routine maintenance.

Opposite Landscape site plan by Jo McProud of McProud & Associates

Above Rendering of the "Temple to Recycling" where residents are encouraged to recycle

Waterbrook Yowie Bay

Yowie Bay (Sydney), New South Wales, Australia
Waterbrook Lifestyle Resorts / Campbell Luscombe Architects

Owner's Statement

Project type Active Senior/
Independent Living Residence

Site location Suburban

Site size 12,188m²

Building footprint 5,443m²

Building area 15,700m²

Date completed February 2001

Photography courtesy of the
architect

The Waterbrook Vision was to revolutionize the concept of retirement village living by offering excellence in design, lifestyle, service, security, and care that is delivered with integrity and professionalism. The client aimed to make the Waterbrook name synonymous with the best in seniors living in Australia and Asia.

The ethos of Waterbrook was to offer to independent senior living a high-quality architectural environment, coupled with the services and facilities that residents would expect to find in a luxury hotel. With very few exceptions, until the launch of Waterbrook Yowie Bay, the retirement living industry in Australia produced a modest and undistinguished product. The industry was largely dominated by "not for profit" organizations or commercial interests catering to the lower end of the market. Waterbrook was to provide high-quality surroundings where residents have maximum choice to pursue an active and stimulating lifestyle, all with the comfort of knowing that if and when care is required, it is discreetly available.

The owner, Waterbrook Lifestyle Resorts, was early to recognize the changing demographic (largely based on Sydney's rising property values) that would provide a market for retirement housing at the higher end of the economic spectrum. They also possessed a shrewd ability in selecting sites close to desirable property features.

Right Entry porte-cochère

Opposite Gardens and watercourse of Waterbrook

Architect's Statement

Waterbrook Yowie Bay introduced the concept of premium resort lifestyle living to the retirement/seniors living industry in Sydney. Set on 3.2 acres (1.3 hectares) of landscaped gardens, the two apartment buildings and the garden clubhouse have been sited to create a series of linked, secluded open spaces, focusing around a man-made, but totally naturalistic landscaped water feature that flows through the length of the resort. Despite being in a typical suburban context, the style of the building, while maintaining a compatible scale with its neighbors, was developed to respond to the aesthetic aspirations and memories of senior residents by utilizing a dignified contemporary interpretation of earlier "grand" classical apartment buildings of the 1920s and '30s.

Despite being a boutique retirement community, the project housed a broad range of amenities for its residents, including an indoor heated swimming pool, a gymnasium, hairdressing salon, meeting rooms, a billiard room, putting green, bowling green, and an à-la-carte restaurant. Even ten years after completion, the 72-unit multiple award-winning serviced independent living development still maintains its leading position as Sydney's premier retirement community. The project won the Retirement Lifestyle award from the Urban Development Institute of Australia (NSW) and was subsequently awarded by the Australian Master Builders Association.

Opposite Grand staircase off entry to Waterbrook
Above The well-equipped, restful library

Client Goals and Design Team Solutions

1 Client goal: The introduction of resort lifestyle living to the retirement/seniors living industry.

Design team solution: The client's image of providing their residents with the ambiance of an elegant 5-star boutique hotel was achieved by creating a combination of a generosity of space and a palette of fine materials and the provision of a lavish level of facilities. The sequence of entry from the street through the porte-cochere into the equivalent of a grand hotel lobby reinforced the character of an upmarket hotel. Corridors were limited in length and a sequence of small, well-appointed lounge areas positioned throughout the buildings that opened onto small outside gardens. The densely landscaped and secluded internal courtyard spaces created an oasis-like separation from the surrounding suburban context.

2 Client goal: Maximize the potential of the site location and create a boutique, prestige retirement development.

Design team solution: The unusually large parcel of established residential land, within the suburban context, (formerly a redundant primary school) in a typical south Sydney suburban setting formed the site. The unrealized potential of the site, which was located within a pleasant tree-lined, low-density suburban street, was however in proximity to more prestigious surrounding waterfront residential properties. The demolition of the former primary school had carefully retained and preserved a number of groupings of significant eucalyptus trees scattered throughout the site. The building design and layout weaved throughout the tree groupings that formed the basis of the lavish landscaped gardens that became the oasis within the resort.

3 Client goal: Continuing care.

Design team solution: As well as providing prestige accommodation, the underlying basis of the project was to offer discrete continuing care services to the resident. It was recognized that the desire of the residents was to retain their independence as long as possible and to avoid the inconvenience of institutionalized care. The management offers (on a pay-as-you-go basis) the ability to bring any necessary care to the apartment. The apartments were designed to accommodate a live-in caregiver. One of the primary elements of care was recognized as the fostering of a vital, socially active community, enhanced by the variety and availability of the recreational and communal facilities.

Major Design Objectives and/or Project Challenges and the Related Responses

1 Architectural character: The project was to attract as much by the quality of its apartments and the variety of its facilities, as by the character of the building itself. The style of the building, a dignified contemporary interpretation of many of the "grand" classical apartment buildings of the 1920's and 30's found in Sydney, was developed to respond to the aesthetic aspirations and cultural memories of its senior residents, particularly those resident in or familiar with the surrounding setting. As well as the recognizable architectural form, the buildings were also to elicit an interior that possessed the light and relaxed ambiance of a resort.

2 The creation of a vibrant community: The core objective was to ensure a vibrant seniors community, not merely a collection of apartments inhabited by elderly people. The two apartment blocks (each with a separate street address) and the recreation pavilion, spatially create a large meandering internal courtyard space. The arrangement of the buildings was designed to retain a sequence of groupings of retained mature eucalyptus trees. The subsequent landscaping structured itself around these large existing trees and gave a density to the planting from the building's opening. Internally, the large, open community spaces form a path throughout the building, always enhancing the opportunity for meeting and social interaction.

3 The garden environment: Hidden within the project are the extensive internal native gardens. They create a private sanctuary not apparent from the street and an illusion of spaciousness beyond their actual dimension. The landscaping maximizes the potential of the significant clusters of mature trees retained during construction, but it is the extraordinarily realistic man-made creek meandering through the gardens that enlivens the project and lend the project its name. The configuration of the buildings creates a sequence of densely linked landscaped courtyards, each with its own character. Covered pathways and bridge crossings link all the buildings and the garden pavilion, which houses many of the amenities. The project's common areas and restaurant as well as many apartments overlook the private gardens.

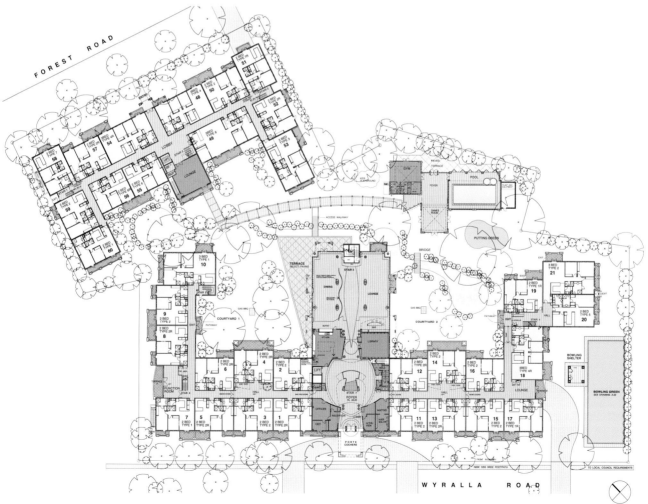

Waterbrook Yowie Bay   205

Unique Context

The southern suburbs of Sydney, and particularly the Sutherland Shire, in which the project is located, while not being far from downtown Sydney, are framed by the ocean to the east, and form the termination of the suburban spread to the south of the city, where the suburbs meet the Royal National Park.

The project sits within a moderately affluent suburban situation, where nearby inland waterways and bays form an attractive setting. The surrounding areas were always envisioned as the market for the project's future residents. But it was to be the return to a substantial classical architectural presence and the beautiful hidden gardens within that were to separate the project from its immediate surroundings and define it as a prestige address. The project was among the earliest retirement living developments in Sydney to recognize the demographic change that saw the cohort of affluent retirees emerging, and remains today a prestige address.

Other Project Information

The initial development team saw the potential for a prestigious seniors community in an area where little had previously been provided. The project was originally composed of two (now three) separate buildings, each addressing a different street, with a garden pavilion clubhouse. Each of the residential buildings comprises two residential stories with basement underground parking for residents and visitors. The residential accommodation is apartment style, with a variety of 1, 2 and 3-bedroom accommodation. The development team was initially surprised by the strong demand for the larger 3-bedroom apartments and the design team amended the layouts to amalgamate smaller apartments together, even during the early stages of construction.

Environmental Sustainability & Energy Conservation

The building reflects an intelligent response to environmental and sustainability issues. The development's ESD strategy maximizes the number of corner apartments with increased access to natural day-lighting and cross-ventilation by maximizing the number of

aspects these apartments address. Passive sustainability, i.e. good orientation, carefully designed sun access and shielding, limit the dependence on mechanical environmental support. Gardens and landscaping are watered from rainwater harvesting stored in tanks formed below the resorts bowling green and reticulated throughout the site.

Advanced Technology

As well as necessary emergency notification access facilities, the project provides residents with all the modern communication and lifestyle technology expected in high-end residential developments.

Design & Philosophy of Care

While the project is an independent living development, the underlying basis of the project was to offer discreet continuing care services to the resident. It was recognized that the desire of the residents was to retain their independence as long as possible and to avoid the inconvenience of institutionalized care. The management offers (on a pay-as-you-go basis) the ability to bring any necessary care to the apartment. The apartments were designed to accommodate a live-in caregiver. One of the primary elements of care was recognized as the fostering of a vital, socially active community, enhanced by the variety and availability of the recreational and communal facilities.

Integration of Residents with the Broader Community

The project, by its location and target market was always intended to attract its residents from the local surrounding area. Subsequently, an easy integration of residents with the broader community was achievable, most living in proximity to their existing cultural, retail, and lifestyle centers.

While being a private community, the public spaces are often opened to the public for community functions, most notably the ground level areas of the entry atrium space and the restaurant and lounge areas are used as a function faculty hosting community and charitable events.

Opposite top The Waterbrook Restaurant
Opposite bottom An apartment interior

Staffing

Total number of staff at this project/facility 5

Number of management staff 2

Number of other staff (e.g. maintenance, housekeeping, food services) 4

Project Capacity and Numbers of Units

Independent living apartments 72

Kitchen (daily meals served) available as required

Fitness/rehab/wellness (daily visits) The facilities include a swimming pool, fitness center, bowling green, and consulting facilities

Pool(s) and related areas (daily visits) Indoor heated swimming pool within the facilities area of the development

Breakdown of Independent Living Units

One-bedroom units 2
Typical size per unit 64m²

Two bedroom units 52
Typical size per unit 96m²

Two bedroom-plus units 18
Typical size per unit 120m²

Resident/Client Age

Current average age approximately 76 years old

Age upon entry approximately 72 years old

Resident/Client Fees and Funding

Entry fee Yes

Client monthly funding Private (out-of-pocket) pay

Public/Government funded No

Public/Government subsidies (means tested based on assets and/or income) No

The population of Waterbrook Yowie Bay is predominately retired couples. Most residents would have been local private business owners. All units are purchased with prices being in the upper percentile of the Sydney real estate market.

Opposite top Bridge connecting the activities pavilion
Opposite bottom Terrace from the Waterbrook Restaurant
Above Watercourse and gardens

Wolf Creek Lodge

Grass Valley, California, USA
Wolf Creek Lodge LLC / McCamant & Durrett Architects

Project type Active Senior/
Independence Living Residence,
Community-Based Services,
Senior Cohousing

Site location Small town

Site size 0.4 hectares

Building footprint 1,135m²

Building area 2,960m²

Total building cost US$4.3 million

Building cost US$1,442/m²

Date completed October 2012

Photography Charles Durrett

Owner's Statement

Wolf Creek Lodge includes 30 one- and two-bedroom independent condominiums. The 325 square meters of common facilities include a large dining room, gourmet kitchen, sitting area with fireplace, laundry, office, crafts rooms, and three guestrooms, one of which may be used as a caregiver quarters. Outside there are community gardens and a spa, as well as 35 parking spaces in a variety of open and garage spaces. The community itself is located on less than half a hectare, and one of the community's attractions is its walkable location, providing easy access to nearby stores and restaurants.

Wolf Creek Lodge was developed by a unique partnership of cohousing community members (the eventual buyers organized as Wolf Creek Lodge LLC) and the professional developer CoHousing Partners LLC. CoHousing Partners began bringing these buyers together through a series of visioning and design workshops.

The residents of Wolf Creek Lodge are a group of independent, active adults who have come together to create a supportive community in which they can age safely and live fully with dignity and humor. The group was inspired by the splendid serene and natural setting, inspiring them to be responsible stewards dedicated to sustaining their physical environment. In a community fostered by patience, open-mindedness, respect, and trust, the residents wanted a co-operative, harmonious way of living, full of laughter and joyful community. Together, they will learn and grow, sharing a strong sense of belonging and a heartfelt experience of coming home.

Right Rendering of Wolf Creek Lodge from the street

Opposite top Rendering of the terrace from a common balcony

Opposite bottom Rendering of the terrace from the entry pathway

Architect's Statement

The overreaching goal with the design of Wolf Creek Lodge was to optimize the community's environmental and social sustainability. The challenging hillside site also presented many unique opportunities: providing a transition from the adjacent commercial areas, defining an important neighborhood street corner while orienting the residences toward the views of surrounding woods. Creating a balance between privacy and community was also important for the residents. Balconies that run along the entire south façade, a central terrace, and a garden court allows them to have their own privacy while also having easy opportunities for spontaneous social interaction.

Architecturally, its hillside site located near lots of amenities inspired the design for Wolf Creek Lodge. The building was pushed to the northeast, defining the street corner to improve the neighborhood's urban design and sense of place, while also taking advantage of the site's walkability. The corner location also reduced construction costs by keeping the building on the hill and off the slope. Its southern orientation not only provides views of the rest of the beautiful property, but embraces the sun, encouraging the use of solar panels and passive heating and cooling techniques.

Above The common terrace showing the East wing
Opposite top The common terrace showing the West wing
Opposite bottom Wolf Creek Lodge grand opening

Client Goals and Design Team Solutions

1 Client Goal: Creating easy opportunities for spontaneous social interaction.

Design team solution: Some of the most valuable social areas are the balcony walkways, which are wide enough for people to furnish in their personal style. Many residents have created sitting areas where they can sit outside their front doors, and often end up chatting with neighbors. In addition, at the end of each wing, on each floor, there is a wider balcony area that serves as larger gathering nodes, which are frequently used by residents to share a cup of coffee or glass of wine.

2 Client Goal: Balancing privacy and community.

Design team solution: Most of the homes in Wolf Creek Lodge have an outdoor sitting area in front of their home, with the kitchen sinks looking out toward the community areas, and a much more private deck on the back side of their homes.

3 Client Goal: Taking advantage of the site's natural setting and views.

Design team solution: The building hugs the street front to give more definition to the corner, and at the same time opens its wings, as if they were open arms, on the opposite side, to take full advantage of the views and breezes coming up from the valley.

Major Design Objectives and/or Project Challenges and the Related Responses

1 Hugging the sun: In a culture that relies heavily on air conditioning, the goal was to reduce that as much as possible. The residents came to a conclusion that air conditioning units would not be placed in their homes, but rather only in the Common House. The design of the building is meant to support this decision and allow the building to be passively heated and cooled.

2 Desuburbanization: Grass Valley, California, is a largely suburbanized town, where a majority of the population lives in single-family homes. It has the highest per-capita rate of seniors living alone. Wolf Creek Lodge aimed to desuburbanize their lives, creating a community where they could live with people they love and trust.

3 Common facilities: As with all cohousing communities, the common house is the hub of the community. There was no exception here. The residents wanted their common house to be an extension of their living room, where they could relax and feel at home. It is completely self-managed, so the residents have to work together to keep it usable for everyone.

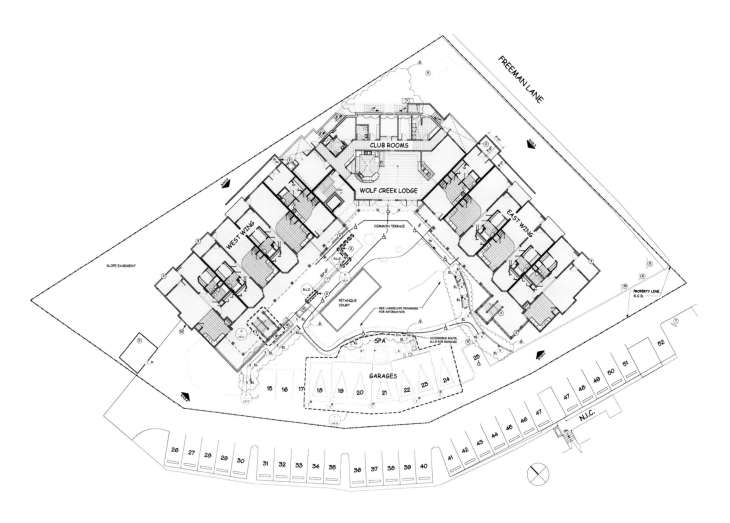

FREEMAN LANE

CLUB ROOMS

WOLF CREEK LODGE

EAST WING

WEST WING

COMMON TERRACE

SLOPE EASEMENT

PROPERTY LINE, S.C.D.

PÉTANQUE COURT

SEE LANDSCAPE DRAWINGS FOR INFORMATION

SPA

ACCESSIBLE ROUTE, B.C.D FOR SIGNAGE

GARAGES

15 16 17 18 19 20 21 22 23 24 25

N.I.C.

47 48 49 50 51 52

41 42 43 44 45 46 47

26 27 28 29 30 31 32 33 34 35 36 37 38 39 40

BEDROOM 1
13'-3" x 11'-0"

4 SHELVES

4 SHELVES

LINEN

laundry/
pantry

BEDROOM 2
10'-6" x 11'-0"

2'-6"

44'-0"

28'-0"

0   7ft

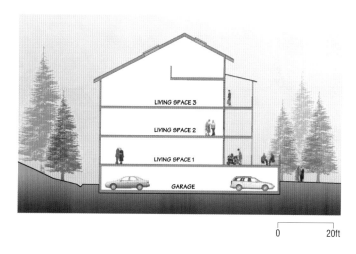

LIVING SPACE 3

LIVING SPACE 2

LIVING SPACE 1

GARAGE

0   20ft

Opposite Solar panels on the Lodge

Top Wolf Creek Lodge building plan

Left Private house floor plan

Above Section through West wing

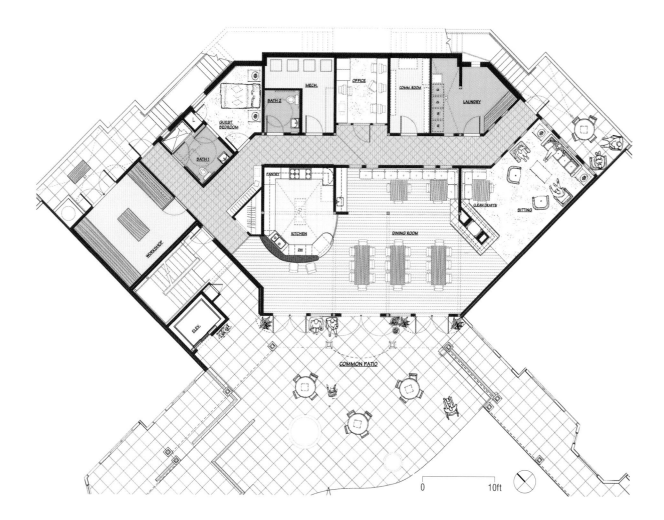

Unique Context

Wolf Creek Lodge was intended, from the very beginning, to be all about fun, reflecting the spirit of the independent, active adults of the group. They have created a supportive community in which to age safely and live fully with dignity and humor.

The proximity of the site to the downtown, in addition to being the first corner on Freeman Lane to be developed, presented a unique opportunity to contribute to the walkability of the neighborhood and the city, a component of a healthy lifestyle that promotes aging-in-place. The outdoor spaces provide plenty of opportunities for interaction, conviviality, and community building.

The Lodge is a community fostered by patience, open-mindedness, respect, and trust. Its residents enjoy a co-operative, harmonious way of living, filled with laughter. It is a joyful, sustainable neighborhood—both socially and environmentally. The Lodge operates 59 per cent above 2008 Title 24 and was awarded Project of the Quarter by California Multi-Family New Homes.

Environmental Sustainability & Energy Conservation

The project employs an array of energy-saving strategies, including tightening the building envelope, optimizing natural daylight, and solar preheated domestic hot water. Careful shading, super-insulation, and ceiling fans provide passive cooling, while increased interior mass, efficient windows, and radiant barriers contribute to passive heating.

Wolf Creek Lodge is the winner of the prestigious California State 2011 Governor's Environmental and Economic Leadership Award for Sustainable Communities. As the fifth senior cohousing community in the United States, the community, its shared open spaces, and its common facilities demonstrate an innovative approach to environmental and social sustainability by creating a neighborhood where seniors can support each other.

Opposite top Wolf Creek Lodge common kitchen
Opposite bottom Residents enjoying a common meal in the dining room
Above Common house floor plan

Advanced Technology

Wolf Creek Lodge was designed to utilize the sun as much as possible. The L-shaped building faces south. All three levels have concrete balconies along the entire front. The wide balconies provide ample shade for the units in the summer. The units are also very open on the interior, with the kitchen, dining, and living room all encumbered into one room. This allows for good ventilation through the unit, allowing the warm air to be flushed out in the evenings. During the winter, the concrete balconies gather the heat from the sun and slowly release it at night.

The design also utilized advanced framing and in-floor radiant heating. These solutions were small moves to keep the building personally and environmentally comfortable. By using advanced framing techniques, 25–40 per cent less lumber was used than a building of the same square meterage. The in-floor radiant heat uses only one boiler for the whole building.

Design & Philosophy of Care

Wolf Creek Lodge can thrive only because the developer and architect worked closely with the buyers' group during the development process. It was during this process that residents got to know each other, created a shared vision for their community, learned to work in a well-functioning committee structure, and ultimately how to manage their own community. The physical structure supports this vision, but it is the strength of the social community and their ability to work together that allows the community to truly thrive.

Integration of Residents with the Broader Community

In addition to providing a fun-loving environment, Wolf Creek Lodge has pioneered the urban design development of the neighborhood. The stance of the building on the site 'holds the corner.' This started an important pioneer effort in weaving the fabric of the town back together while also making it senior-friendly.

Residents can safely walk to shopping across the street. Grass Valley's historic center is only 15 minutes away, providing a wide variety of other shops, restaurants, and landmarks.

The open space on the site functions as a gathering node for neighbors to engage in different activities, such as pétanque and gardening, which enhances the vacation-like feel of the community.

Opposite top Common balconies leading to private house units
Opposite bottom One resident's personalization of the balcony in front of their unit
Below A gathering on the common balcony

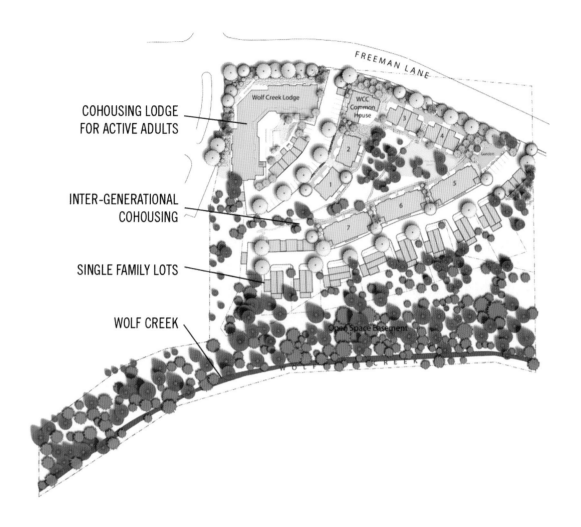

COHOUSING LODGE
FOR ACTIVE ADULTS

INTER-GENERATIONAL
COHOUSING

SINGLE FAMILY LOTS

WOLF CREEK

FREEMAN LANE

Staffing

Total number of staff at the facility None, but it is designed to welcome a caregiver at a later date

Number of management staff Wolf Creek Lodge is completely self-managed

Number of care staff (registered nursing and direct care staff) None, but the facility is designed to welcome a caregiver at a later date

Direct care hours per day per client Currently none, except for neighbors

Project Capacity and Numbers of Units

Independent living apartments 30

Assisted living cottages/villas As required

Special care for persons with dementia As required

Skilled nursing care (beds) As required

Kitchen (daily meals served) As required

Elder day care (clients) As required

Breakdown of Independent Living Units

One bedroom units 12
Typical size per unit 58m²

Two bedroom units 18
Typical size per unit 95m²

Resident/Client Age

Current average age 55 to 80 years

Resident/Client Fees and Funding

Entry fee or unit purchase Yes

Client Monthly Funding Private (out-of-pocket) pay

Residents range from 55 to 80 years old. They are and have been very active members of the larger community. Many of them have been caregivers, and seek a caring, giving, co-operative environment for caregivers. There are no staff at Wolf Creek Lodge. The community is self-managed, where the residents rely on each other and neighbors for any other support. However, the cohousing was designed to accommodate caregivers at any given time.

Opposite top A resident watering the common garden beds
Opposite bottom The residents themselves completed the landscaping
Above Wolf Creek Lodge context plan

Index of architects

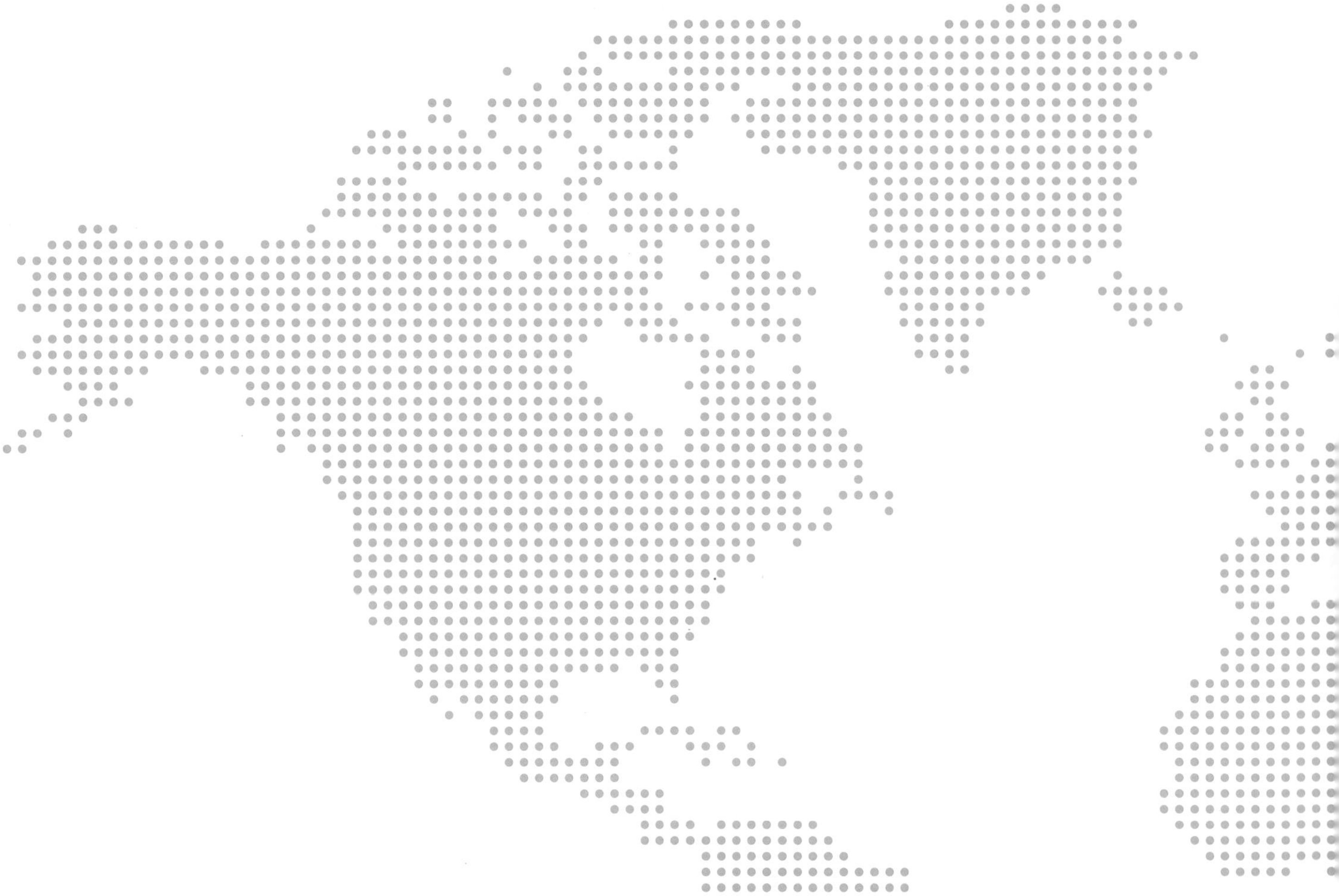

THE GLO